VOGUE

FITTING

The book of fitting techniques,
adjustments, and alterations

PERENNIAL LIBRARY

HARPER & ROW, PUBLISHERS, NEW YORK

Cambridge, Philadelphia, San Francisco, Washington
London, Mexico City, São Paulo, Singapore, Sydney

Writer: *Sandra Lenker*

Illustrator: *Phoebe Gaughan*

Editor: *Helen Moore*

Coordinator for Butterick: *Patricia Perry*

Butterick Staff: *Jane Glanzer, Carol Sharma, Renee Ullman*

Coordinator for Harper & Row: *Carol Cohen*

Harper & Row production staff: *Mary Chadwick, Lydia Link, Coral Tysliava*

A hardcover edition of this book is published by Harper & Row, Publishers, Inc.

VOGUE FITTING. Copyright © 1984 by Butterick Company, Inc. All rights reserved. Printed in the United States of America. No part of this book may be used or reproduced in any manner whatsoever without written permission except in the case of brief quotations embodied in critical articles and reviews. For information address Harper & Row, Publishers, Inc., 10 East 53rd Street, New York, N.Y. 10022. Published simultaneously in Canada by Fitzhenry & Whiteside Limited, Toronto.

First PERENNIAL LIBRARY edition published 1987

Designed by Betty Bins Graphics

Library of Congress Cataloging-in-Publication Data
Main entry under title:

Vogue fitting.

"Perennial Library."
Includes index.
"Based on the Vogue sewing book of fitting, adjustments, and alterations"—
T.p. verso.
1. Dressmaking. 2. Tailoring (Women's). 3. Clothing and dress—Alteration.
I. Vogue sewing book of fitting, adjustments, and alterations.
TT515.V623 1987 646.4'304 84-47561
IBSN 0-06-091410-6 (pbk.)

87 88 89 90 91 FG 10 9 8 7 6 5 4 3 2 1

Other books from Vogue

VOGUE SEWING

VOGUE CHRISTMAS

VOGUE DOLLS & TOYS

VOGUE EASY SEWING

VOGUE SEWING FOR THE HOME

VOGUE SEWING FOR YOUR CHILDREN

Contents

Introduction

Congratulations! You have taken the first positive step toward perfecting your fitting skills. You are about to learn a logical, step-by-step, professional fitting method that will guide you through the tough spots and reinforce what you may already know.

Vogue Fitting will help you understand your body and your individual fitting requirements. It will give you the expertise to create a well-fitted garment and a more pleasing image. Chapters 1 and 2 will give you the necessary knowledge to select a pattern style and size that is right for your body.

Vogue Fitting approaches adjustments and alterations in three distinct sections, each serving a specific purpose. Chapter 3, "Pattern Tissue Adjustments," offers you detailed instructions on the first phase of pattern adjustments: those done on the tissue pattern before you cut the fashion fabric. They are based on your measurements and their variations from the standard body measurements.

Chapter 4, "The Basic Fitting Shell," shows how to make a fitting shell. Alterations are made on the fitting shell and then transferred to the pattern tissue. In the process you will produce a master pattern that is adapted to your body contours. *Vogue Fitting* will show you how to use this pattern as a fitting tool for all other fashion patterns you sew.

The final fitting chapter, "Refining the Fit," gives instructions for making alterations directly on your fashion garment. For those who choose not to make a fitting shell, this is the first stage of alterations to the garment in a three-dimensional form. For those who do make a fitting shell, it offers invaluable information for refining the fit of each individual garment as it evolves from fabric to fashion.

Vogue Fitting has combined all the fitting information for pants into one chapter. So, for those of you who are interested specifically in pants fitting, these same three fitting stages are explained in one section—conveniently and without extraneous information.

The Vogue Basic Fitting Shell #1004 is a tissue pattern used for making a fitting shell. The fitting shell can be a perfect sewing tool to save you time and trouble every time you sew; use it to check for potential fitting problems before cutting your fabric.

The Vogue Professional Fitting Program #1001 includes a specially designed master pattern printed on non-woven fabric for use in making a fitting shell. Also included with the package is a step-by-step booklet explaining how to adjust and alter the master pattern plus exclusive fitting tools to help perfect your fitting skills.

Vogue Fitting is based on the premise that you already have basic sewing knowledge. References are made periodically to *Vogue Sewing,* and there are many additional places where *Vogue Sewing* could help you brush up your knowledge. Use the two books together as a complete sewing and fitting encyclopedia—picking and choosing the information that will help you create more beautiful garments and a more beautiful you.

1 Getting Started

Elements Influencing Fit

The fit of a garment is influenced by a variety of factors including the design, the fabric you choose, the undergarments you wear, and the accuracy of your sewing. All these elements can be controlled or altered to accommodate the goal of a perfect fit. Your body, the one factor over which you have only limited control, also has an important effect on the fit of a garment. Your posture and body proportions will determine how a pattern based on standard measurements will take shape on you.

The following pages will take you through the exercises that will help you analyse your body objectively. An awareness of your body proportions, both length and width, can help you select styles that flatter your figure as well as avoid unnecessary alterations. This is the first step toward a perfect fit.

POSTURE

Today's fashionable woman strives for a healthy image; good posture is crucial to completing that image. Posture communicates your attitude about yourself and about the world. The pride and poise that come with self-assurance will do much to aid your posture. Good posture is an expression of good physical and mental fitness.

Good posture is also natural, in that it is comfortable and healthful for the body. The rigid or extremely erect figure produces tension and strain, especially in the knees and back muscles. It shortens the distance from back of neck to shoulder blades, and lengthens the distance from base of neck to apex of bust, thereby causing fitting problems. The opposite of this rigid

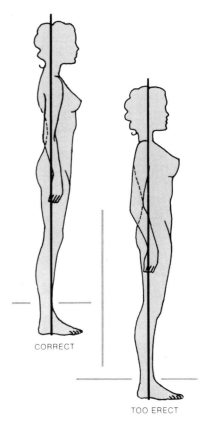

CORRECT

TOO ERECT

posture is the slump. Slumping with the chin thrust forward, the chest sunken, and the stomach protruding will produce rounded shoulders, fatigue, and backache. Dowager's hump, sway back, and protruding abdomen are fitting problems that may evolve from slumping.

Naturally, you are wondering how your own compares to the illustration of good posture. To test this, stand with your back against a wall and your weight resting on your feet. If posture is correct, your shoulders, shoulder blades, and buttocks should touch the wall; you should barely be able to insert your hand between the wall and the small of the back. If only your shoulders touch the wall, your posture is too erect. If only your shoulder blades touch, you are round-shouldered.

The pull of gravity causes additional posture and health problems for the woman who is overweight. Being overweight causes redistribution of the weight so that it does not fall in a plumb line over the kneecap and the arch of the foot. This can cause foot problems as well as backache. Excess weight also strains the muscles so that they cannot hold the chest, stomach, and buttocks in their proper positions; these areas then sag. The strain on the entire frame can cause a reduction in height, since the excess weight is pulling down and straining the muscles, which are unable to hold the body erect against the pull of gravity. This downward pull on the body reduces height and inevitably leads to slumping. The compact figure without excess weight can maintain the muscular tension necessary to hold the organs and their surrounding flesh in place without strain, and can thus stand at full height comfortably. The overweight woman must work harder to stand up straight and is often unsuccessful because of her bulk.

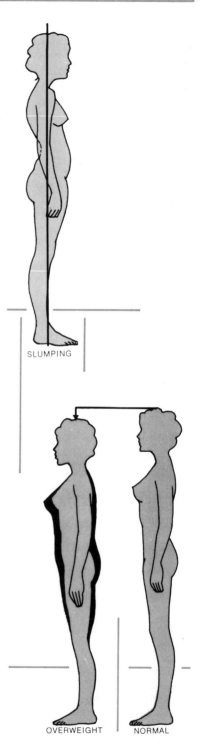

SLUMPING

OVERWEIGHT   NORMAL

PROPORTION

Proportion is the space relationships among the various parts of your body. Your goal is to achieve visually pleasing divisions that enhance your total image. Understanding your own body proportions and how they relate to an ideal is essential before you can use fashion designs to create flattering images and illusions. The ideally proportioned body is composed of four basic factors:

☐ Half the length of the body is above the fullest part of the hip and half below the fullest part of the hip.

☐ The waist falls halfway between the underarm and the fullest part of the hip.

☐ The lower half of the body is divided at the knees.

☐ Elbows fall at the waist; fingertips fall at mid-thigh.

12

Measuring your length proportions

You can measure your body according to the following directions. Then fill in your own measurements and compare the results to the ideal. Understanding your differences will help you choose designs that will flatter your figure. To begin, tie a string around the fullest part of your hips, another around your waist, and a third around your torso under your arms.

Overall body proportion Measure from the top of the head to the floor (without shoes). Divide this measurement in half. Measure from the top of the head to the fullest part of the hip. Compare this measurement to your height divided in half. The ideal proportion is to have the hips fall at the midpoint of your total body length. If your hip measurement is longer than half your height, then your body length is greater above your hips. If this measurement is shorter than half your height, then your body length is greater below your hips.

Upper body proportion Measure from the underarm to the fullest part of the hip. Divide this measurement in half. Measure from the underarm to the waist. Compare these measurements. The ideal proportion is to have the waist fall halfway between the underarm and the fullest part of the hip. If your waist measurement is longer than half your underarm-to-hip measure-

ment, you are long waisted; if shorter, you are short waisted.

Lower body proportion Measure from the fullest part of the hip to the floor (without shoes). Divide this measurement in half. Measure from the fullest part of the hip to the knee. Compare these measurements. If your knee measurement is longer than half the hip-to-floor measurement, your length is greater in your thighs. If shorter, it is greater in your calves. The ideal proportion is to have the calf length 1"–2" (2.5cm–5cm) longer than the thigh length.

Arm proportion to body length Hold your arms at your sides. The ideal proportion is to have your elbows fall at your waistline, and your fingertips at the middle of your thighs. If your fingertips fall below the middle of your thighs, you have proportionally long arms; if they fall above, you have short arms.

LENGTH PROPORTIONS

Head to floor_____

Head to hips_____

Underarm to hips_____

Underarm to waist_____

Hips to floor_____

Hips to knee_____

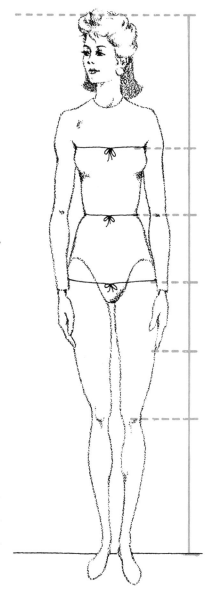

13

Measuring your width proportions

WIDTH PROPORTIONS

Bust_____

Waist_____

Hips_____

Just as the length measurements helped you evaluate your length proportions, a few circumference measurements will help you evaluate your width proportions.

Measure your body at three positions—the bust, waist, and hips. In general, the ideal width proportion is to have the bust and hips measure almost the same and the waist measure approximately 10" (25.5cm) smaller.

Determine from these circumference measurements whether you are full or small busted, thin or thick waisted, heavy or small hipped.

Evaluating your proportions

FEATURES TO BE CAMOUFLAGED

_____
_____
_____
_____
_____
_____

FEATURES TO BE EMPHASIZED

_____
_____
_____
_____
_____
_____

Once you have completed all the measurements, take a good look at your figure in a full-length mirror, wearing only underwear or, even better, a leotard or body suit. Examine your silhouette from all angles—front, back, and side. Be honest with your evaluation and note any additional figure features. Do you have a long or short neck? Are your shoulders narrow, broad, or sloping? Do you have thin arms or thick elbows? Your visual evaluation combined with the comparison of your length and width proportions will help you create a more beautiful image.

Now that you have a clear picture of your body, make a list of the features you want to emphasize and those you wish to camouflage.

Your goal is to create your most flattering image based on your own body proportions. To achieve this, learn to use design elements that make your figure features most closely resemble the ideal length and width proportions. The following section on creating illusions will help you achieve that goal.

□ Do you have narrow hips? Then wear full, gathered skirts and designs with yokes to broaden the image in the hip area.

□ Are you thick waisted? If so, choose semi-fitted or loose-fitted designs without waistline definition. If it can't be seen, it can't look bad.

□ Are you flat chested? Blousey bodices and full sleeves are a good choice for you. The excess fabric in loose-fitted designs will create a more flattering illusion.

□ Do you have sloped shoulders? Avoid raglan sleeves, which only emphasize the slope. Choose designs with a well-defined shoulder and a full sleeve; gathering at or on the sleeve cap will conceal the slope.

Creating Illusions

Your goal is to create an image of balance and proportion. That may involve nothing more than dressing your figure, but for most of us who have less than perfect bodies, it will involve creating illusions. The ability to create flattering illusions simply involves executing some basic art and design principles. The knowledge you have gained so far about your body proportions combined with the following information on design principles will help you make the most of what you have.

SILHOUETTES

A silhouette is the basic outline or contour of a garment—the shape of the design. The varieties are endless, but each design originates from a basic design silhouette such as the princess, blouson, A-line, tunic, or shirtwaist. Choose silhouettes that flatter your body proportions.

Waistless silhouettes Designs without waistline seams make a figure appear taller, camouflage the waistline and slim down a broad figure.

A-line A-line designs camouflage broad hips, create a more flattering proportion for a figure with a large bosom, and camouflage a high or low waistline.

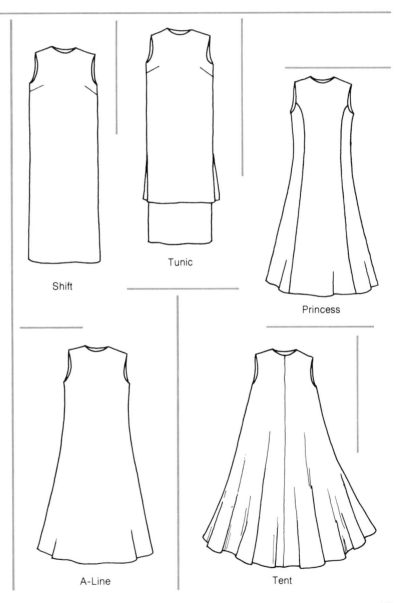

Shift

Tunic

Princess

A-Line

Tent

High-waisted silhouettes An empire design or a silhouette with a bodice yoke makes the figure appear shorter, emphasizes and adds width to the shoulder area, emphasizes and makes a bust appear larger, disguises the waistline and hips, and broadens a thin frame.

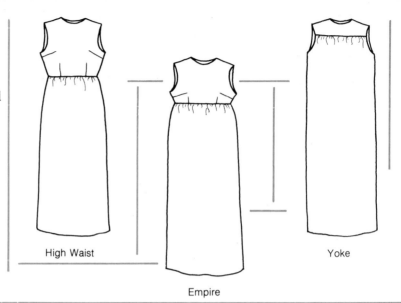

High Waist

Empire

Yoke

Low-waisted silhouettes A low-waisted silhouette emphasizes and adds width to the hip area, makes the figure appear shorter, and camouflages the waistline.

Blouson A fuller silhouette such as this can make the figure appear shorter, add fullness to a bosom, make a long-waisted figure appear more flattering, and add fullness to a thin frame.

Waistline silhouettes Designs with a waistline seam will make an average figure appear balanced or emphasize a figure that is high waisted or low waisted.

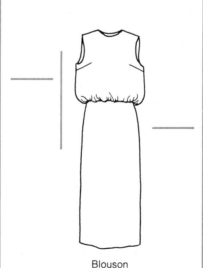

Low Waist

Blouson

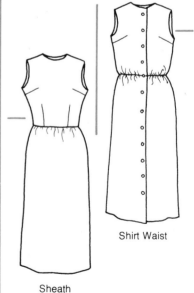

Shirt Waist

Sheath

PROPORTION

Illusions are created by the position of lines on your body; seamlines, hemlines, and fabric designs are all examples of lines that create the illusion of different proportions. They can enhance flattering proportions or minimize those that are unflattering. The print design and texture of the fabric can also

create an image of your choice. Learn to use fabric designs to create proportions that are flattering to your body.

Line

Seams create line images. Fabric designs with lines such as stripes and plaids can also be used to create images and illusions. Our eyes are conditioned to move with lines: long, wide, and bright lines are more dominant than short,

narrow, and dull lines; horizontal lines are more dominant than vertical lines; and curved lines are softer and more relaxed than straight lines.

Thus lines often play tricks with our eyes and create illusions; you want those illusions to work for and not against you.

Fabric design

Small prints and fine textures tend to recede, thus not increasing the apparent size of any figure area. Large prints and thick, heavily textured fabrics tend to advance, creating an illusion of a larger figure size.

Vertical lines To appear taller and thinner, choose designs with the strong effect of a vertical seam, which leads the eye in an up-and-down direction. Single verticals give the greatest impression of height; when they are repeated at even intervals across the garment such as

with vertical stripes, the illusion of length is blunted because our eyes tend to move sideways from line to line as well.

Horizontal lines Horizontal lines emphasize width, although placing a single horizontal seam above or below the median of the body can create an illusion of length throughout the longer area. Since horizontal lines are the strongest ones, avoid designs with horizontal seams or stripes at unflattering locations on your body, such as at a too full bust or too heavy thighs.

Diagonal lines The effect of diagonal lines depends primarily upon the angle and length of the seam or stripe. A short diagonal line that is more horizontal than vertical will lead the eye from side to side, giving an impression of width, whereas a longer line that is more vertical than horizontal leads the eye downward and sideways for a long, narrow look.

Curved lines Curved lines create the same illusion as straight lines but in a less obvious manner. Curved seams also emphasize the curves of the body by repetition, making them more defined. Many times a seam that would be un-

flattering if straight can be nicely worn if modified by a curve. A curved bodice seam or front closing will be softer visually than a straight horizontal or vertical seam.

Hem length

The length of your hem adds one more dimension to your total silhouette—another means by which you can create an illusion that works to your advantage. Hem length is influenced by fashion, but the strongest consideration should be your figure. Lengths that are fashionable on the ideally proportioned body may be di-

sastrous on yours. Sometimes a minor adjustment in the position of the hem can make a world of difference in the visual proportions of your figure. A discriminating eye is your best judge when choosing a hem length that is most flattering to you.

Long, mid-calf lengths can create an image of height and flatter many figures, but they can also have the opposite effect on a short figure by producing proportions that are unbalanced, giving a short-waisted or bottom-heavy appearance.

Avoid having the hem fall at an unattractive position on your leg: the horizontal line will attract the eye and emphasize any undesirable features such as heavy thighs or bony knees.

Above-the-knee hem lengths should be reserved for figures that are slender and/or tall, since they will tend to shorten and broaden the figure. And above all, they should be worn only by those who are fortunate enough to have attractive legs.

COLOR

Color is one of the most obvious elements that affect your total image. Thus a fashion-conscious woman must be aware of the principles of color and the effects and illusions color can produce. An understanding of what color can do for you offers an opportunity to help you look your loveliest.

Color can reflect and influence a multitude of moods. Some colors are cheerful, vivacious, and active; others are restful, serene, and dignified. Some lift spirits and others subdue them.

Color can create illusions. It can create impressions of size, allowing you to use it to your advantage if you understand its effects. Dark and/or dull colors tend to recede, reducing apparent

figure size. Light and/or bright colors tend to advance, making your figure appear larger.

Warm colors—reds, yellows, and oranges—increase the apparent size of the figure; cool colors—blues, greens, and violets—make the figure appear smaller.

Bold, contrasting colors give the illusion of a larger size; subtler color schemes will make the figure appear more compact. When using contrasting colors, the eye is naturally drawn to the brighter color, so if you want to distract the eye from a less desirable figure feature, use a subtler color in that area.

Always take your coloring and personal preferences into consideration, too. Analyze the effect the color has in relation to your skin, hair, and eyes. Sometimes a slight change in shade will make all the difference. And always choose colors you like. If you feel good, you are much more likely to look good.

The manipulation of color is not only one of the most artistic elements of fashion sewing; it is also one of the most exciting. Experiment with it . . . go on a creative fling to create a more colorful you.

MAKING IT WORK FOR YOU

You have measured, analyzed, and evaluated your body, compared it to standards and ideals, and either accepted or changed through posture or diet the curves and contours of your figure.

Armed with the knowledge of how to use color, proportion, and design silhouettes to create illusions, you have the ability to conceal or reveal whatever figure characteristics you choose.

Your goal is to create a more pleasing image, so use your knowledge to make the best of what you have.

□ *Do you have a flat derriere?* Avoid hip-hugging designs that emphasize the lack of fullness. Choose skirt and pant silhouettes that have soft gathers built into the design.

□ *Do you have heavy thighs?* Keep your skirt lengths long enough to hide the problem. Choose designs that fit loosely around the thighs, eliminating the possibility of exposing thigh bulge.

□ *Are your shoulders narrow?* Tent shapes and designs with asymmetrical closings would not be flattering. Choose designs that widen the shoulder area, such as those with yokes, puffed sleeves, or blouson tops. Also, shoulder pads are a good way to increase shoulder width.

□ *Do you have a large bosom?* Avoid designs with a high waist or blouson tops. Concentrate on simple silhouettes such as shirtwaists, shifts, and A-lines.

□ *Are you short waisted?* Any waistless silhouettes like the shift are flattering, as well as designs that have a raised or lowered waist seam. Avoid blouson silhouettes.

Fabrics and Fit

Fabrics are the inspiration for many designs, both in the workrooms of ready-to-wear manufacturers and in your private sewing space at home. The woman who sews is an artist who can choose fabrics and designs that will combine to make a garment she will be proud to wear. A wise seamstress understands the strong influence fabric can have on the finished garment—including the fit. She benefits by a basic understanding of the fibers, structure, and finishes, all of which contribute to the individual characteristics of a wide range of fabrics.

The fabric, with its characteristics, will lend its personality to the design. The same pattern made in two different types of fabrics will not only appear different, but may fit differently as well.

Each detail of its past—the fiber, structure, finishes, etc.—offers a clue to the way the fabric ultimately feels, looks, and behaves. Learn to distinguish fabric characteristics and quality by a thorough understanding of the components that have combined to create it, and you will be one step closer to the custom fit you are seeking.

The chart on pages 24–25 describes the characteristics and fitting considerations of each specific type of fabric. Refer to it as you approach each sewing project.

FIBERS

Fibers are the basic components of fabric, each with its unique characteristics. Fibers fall into two categories: natural and synthetic. Natural fibers are those that originate from natural sources, and synthetic fibers come from manmade sources. Although its properties may be altered by structure and finishes, ultimately a fabric's origin and chemistry are its soul.

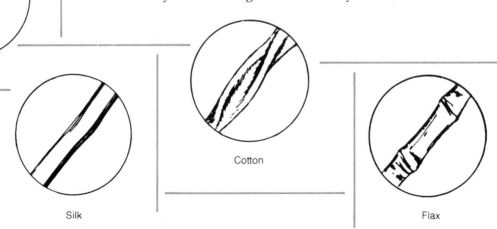

Wool

Silk

Cotton

Flax

Natural

Natural fibers originate from natural sources. Animal, vegetable, and mineral substances all provide the raw material for cloth. The wool of sheep, the hair and fur of other creatures, the fine filament of the silkworm, the fibrous stalk of the flax plant, and the puff of the cotton plant all provide the beginnings of a wide array of beautiful fabrics. Mineral sources provide the fibers for asbestos and certain luxury fabrics such as metallics.

The unmistakable characteristics of natural fibers are borne in their structure. The familiar warmth of wool, the downy softness of cotton, the rich dry texture of silk, and the crisp sheen of linen originate in the plant or animal from which they were made. The irregularities inherent in natural fibers contribute to their beauty.

Synthetic

All synthetic fibers begin as chemical solutions; they are the product of modern technology. Synthetic fibers have offered us a whole new range of fabrics with refined properties and have become indispensable in the contemporary world.

Each type of synthetic fiber has a generic name, such as nylon or polyester. In turn, fiber manufacturers have trademarks or brand names for the various fibers they produce.

Great advances have been made in the development of synthetic fibers since their inception. Today synthetic fibers can be engineered specifically to create fabrics with a wide range of uses and characteristics.

STRUCTURE

The method by which the fabric is formed affects its characteristics. A great variety of methods have been developed over the centuries, and more recently through modern technology, but most fabrics are the result of two basic processes: weaving and knitting. Other processes, including netting, felting, braiding, malimo, and fusing, are responsible for many special modern-day fabrics.

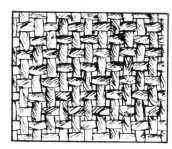

Plain Weave

Wovens

Woven fabrics are produced by the interlacing of yarns—the warp and the weft. There are three basic weaves: plain, twill, and satin. Most other types are a variation of these.

Woven fabrics have a selvage running lengthwise along each edge. Always be certain the crosswise yarns are at a right angle to the selvage; this indicates that the fabric is "on grain," an important consideration in fitting.

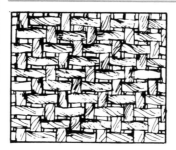

Twill Weave

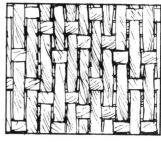

Satin Weave

Knits

Knit fabrics are made up of a series of interlocking loops, either knitted or purled, that results in a flexible construction. Knits generally have a stretchability factor that is not inherent in wovens, although the amount and direction of the stretch varies considerably. This stretch, as well as the evenness of the knit, is an important consideration in fitting.

Plain Knit

Purl Knit

FINISHES

Fabrics are often treated many times throughout their construction. Before they are sold they may have been treated chemically, brushed, glazed, beaten, and polished. Many treatments serve a functional purpose by improving resistance to static, staining, shrinking, wrinkling, or burning. Others, such as napping or brushing, are a step in the process of developing a specific texture. And dyeing and printing are finish treatments creating design characteristics. For more information on fabrics and fabric finishes, see *Vogue Sewing* or your basic sewing book.

CHARACTER

In order to fit your garments to professional standards it is essential that you understand the "personality" of each fabric you use. The fiber, structure, and finish make up the individual characteristics of each fabric, but you must be able to recognize those characteristics and understand how they relate to your body and your design as you strive for a custom fit.

Choosing the correct fabric for the design is one of the most critical decisions you will make as you embark on a sewing project. Refer to the back of your pattern envelope or to the pattern catalogue for the types of fabrics that are appropriate for the design. Always buy quality fabrics; the time and effort you put into a sewing project will be rewarded many times over by the superior results you will obtain. Price is not always the best determinant of quality; you must learn to judge fabrics by their appearance and feel. Although experience is your best teacher, you will find that *Vogue Sewing* contains valuable information on fabrics.

Your reaction when you touch a fabric will provide a first indication of the character of that fabric. We know instinctively whether a fabric is soft or crisp, light or heavy, smooth or textured, loose or firm—an observation referred to as the "hand" of the fabric.

Take a length of the fabric and hold it freely, allowing it to fall and move of its own will. The way it hangs and falls into folds is called the "drape" of the fabric.

Both these factors—hand and drape—will tell you much about the fabric. They are an immediate means by which you can judge the personality and quality of a fabric.

Everything about the fabric influences its character and no one factor is more important than another. Some fibers are by nature more supple and pliable than others, but each can have a wide range of hands. For instance, cotton can be woven into fabric as delicate as a Swiss handkerchief or strong enough to sail a boat; a fine wool challis can be lightweight and soft, whereas a wool flannel can be heavy enough to keep its wearer warm on cold winter days.

The structure can create a fabric as soft and loose as a sweater knit or as crisp and firm as a fine gabardine.

Custom-Fitting Fabrics

FABRIC	CHARACTERISTICS	SPECIAL FITTING INSTRUCTIONS
Fabrics with Give Knits such as double knits, single knits, rib knits, tricot, raschel, jerseys, stretch terry, stretch wovens such as stretch denims, and Lycra* Spandex blends	Have built-in stretchability on the crosswise grain and sometimes on the lengthwise grain as well; have a tendency to cling to the body.	Stretch knit fabrics should be reserved for patterns designed for stretchable knits. Patterns designed for stretchable knits rely on the give of the fabric for comfort and mobility, therefore have less wearing ease built into them. May be necessary to reinforce shoulders and waistline seams to prevent unwanted stretch.
Fabrics with Surface Style Napped or pile fabrics such as corduroy, terry cloth, velvet, velveteen, fleece, melton, velour	Will have a nap or one-way design; can be soft or crisp; often bulky.	If fabric is bulky, cut wider seam allowances to allow for adjustments. Excess fullness may have to be removed from sleeve caps and other eased areas.
Fabrics with Surface Style Fur or furlike fabrics	High-napped fabric often with stiff backing; varying amounts of texture and bulk.	Not appropriate for involved designs; choose pattern carefully; cut wider seam allowances to allow for adjustments. A fitting shell is recommended.
Fabrics That Flow and Float Sheers, lace, crepe de chine, challis, georgette	Lightweight; drapable; soft.	Need loose-fitting designs for fabric to drape; choose patterns accordingly. Because fabrics are delicate, do not overfit. Test for pin marks.
Fabrics with Luster Satin, taffeta, brocade, metallics, beaded and sequined fabric, moiré	Can be soft or crisp; many unravel easily.	Avoid overhandling to prevent unraveling. Choose patterns with few seams. A test garment cut from the fashion pattern could be an aid in close-fitting styles. Do not overfit as fabric will show stress or pull marks.
Fabrics with Special Designs Plaids, stripes, border prints, large design motifs, bias prints	Can be soft or crisp; design of fabric will limit pattern selection.	Plaids, horizontal stripes, and border prints must be positioned on the fabric so that seams and hems match appropriately. Draw the outline of the design on the tissue pattern for correct placement. Avoid designs with an excessive number of seams when using large prints.

FABRIC	CHARACTERISTICS	SPECIAL FITTING INSTRUCTIONS
Fabrics Cut on the Bias		
Bias-cut fabric	Drapes and folds gracefully; can be clingy; stretches easily.	Hang basted garment for 24 hours before fitting. Loose-fitting designs work best. Do not overfit because stress will cause pulls and weaken the garment seams.
Suede, Leather and Leatherlike Fabrics		
Leather and suede—natural and synthetic, vinyl, ciré	May be smooth, shiny or textured. Suede has nap. Little or no give to the fabric; limited drapability.	Surface can be marred with pins; may be necessary to join with paper clips for fitting. Avoid close-fitting designs and styles with intricate seaming. A muslin of the fashion pattern could be helpful with fitted designs.
Fabrics Used for Inner Construction		
Underlining	Lightweight; soft; drapable.	Must be compatible with fashion fabric in care requirements, weight and hand. Must be adjusted identically to the garment. Must mold to the inside of the garment and not interfere with the overall fit. Fit the garment with the underlining in position.
Interfacing	Can be woven or non-woven, fusible or nonfusible. Available in various weights.	Interfacing must be adjusted similarly to the garment at any coordinating positions where adjustments have been made. Must be compatible with the garment in care requirements, weight and hand.
Interlining	Adds warmth to the garment; can be soft and smooth or bulky.	Adds bulk to the garment; therefore cut wider seam allowances to allow for alterations. Refer to information on bulky linings, page 157. If pattern calls for an interlining, be aware that extra room has been allowed. Always fit the garment with the basted interlining in place.
Lining	Smooth, lightweight, soft or crisp.	Must be adjusted identically to the garment; can aid in the fit of a garment because it prevents the garment from clinging to the body.

*DuPont registered trademark

2 Fitting Fundamentals

Fitting Methods

All patterns are designed around standard body measurements. You have learned how to choose a pattern style that best suits your figure. The knowledge you have gained about your figure and about the illusions you can create with color, line, and design may be the most effective fitting tool you have. In fact, this information may be all you need to sew new garments that accommodate your figure characteristics.

But chances are that your pattern will fit you well in certain areas and not in others. Now you need to learn how to measure your body, how to select the proper size and how to adjust the pattern so its proportions fit your body exactly.

There are several ways to approach this. If the differences between your figure and the pattern measurements are simple ones, you can check the pattern you are working on and simply make the adjustments on the pattern tissue before cutting your fabric.

However, you may have a long list of adjustments that you know from experience are almost always necessary, whatever the design. These, too, you would make on the tissue before cutting out the pieces, but they may also involve making further alterations on the fabric itself after the garment is sewn.

If you are uncertain about the cause of your fitting problems and are unsure of how to correct them, you may choose to make a fitting shell. This technique gives you the opportunity to evaluate your figure and solve these problems, and you will then have a master pattern for future reference.

Another option is a test garment, reserved for situations that require attention to the details of a specific design.

The wise seamstress will be discriminating with the process she chooses to achieve a custom fit. Unnecessary adjustments and alterations not only extend the time you spend on a project, but also increase the chances of error. The best approach is to keep it simple, do only what is necessary to achieve a fit that is comfortable and flattering, and enjoy your garments.

26

PATTERN TISSUE ADJUSTMENTS

The first stage in fitting involves pattern tissue adjustments—those basic length and circumference changes that are made on the tissue pattern before the garment is cut from your fashion fabric. Minor differences can most often be handled with a simple understanding of these fundamental adjustments.

ALTERATIONS

The second stage in fitting involves alterations that are made on the fitting shell or garment after it is basted together. Certain fabrics and designs may create a need for different alterations in order to achieve the refined fit for which you are striving.

THE FITTING SHELL

The decision whether or not to make a fitting shell will be made on the basis of your previous experiences with fitting, your knowledge of your figure and how to accommodate its specific characteristics, and your sewing skills.

The purpose of a fitting shell is to analyze your fitting problems, determine the cause, and establish a solution. If you have already done that without the aid of a fitting shell, then the process becomes unneces-

sary. If, however, your fitting experiences have been frustrating and unsuccessful, the time invested in making a fitting shell may well be the most rewarding in your sewing experience. It will be a new and positive beginning for future sewing projects and will provide you with a fitting tool that will be the basis for the fit of every garment you make.

In order for a fitting shell to be effective, it must be sewed with care; therefore it is not a project to be undertaken by a novice. If you are a beginning sewer, gain some technical experience first with projects that do not require extensive fitting. Vogue #1001 will take you step-by-step through the fitting process.

TEST GARMENTS

Complicated designs and expensive fabrics, combined with a figure that requires involved modifications, may occasion the need for a test garment. For this purpose, make all the pattern adjustments you would normally make for a specific design, then sew it first in an inexpensive fabric that is comparable in weight and characteristics to your fashion fabric. This provides an opportunity to perfect the fit before you cut into expensive fabric or make irreparable errors on complicated designs. As you sew and expand your fitting knowledge, you should develop enough skill and confidence to reserve this procedure for only the most select situations.

ALTERNATIVE SOLUTIONS

A fitting problem is normally solved through adjustments and alterations, but don't exclude other solutions as well. Perhaps your choice of design needs to be evaluated. If you have continually had unsuccessful results with a particular type of design, it may not be appropriate for your figure. Review the information on creating illusions and design selection on pages 15–18.

Sometimes a pattern adjustment will accentuate a fitting problem and create an unflattering image. In that case, a better solution is to change the appearance of your body proportions rather than adjust the pattern to accommodate the characteristics. For instance, sloped shoulders are sometimes better handled by simply adding shoulder pads. A change of undergarments could be the answer: A different bra design might end the need for a bust adjustment and be more flattering as well. Overly tight underwear might be producing a thigh bulge that would disappear with a different size or style.

Consider the alternatives as you evaluate your adjustment needs. The purpose is to avoid unnecessary adjustments, and to create the most flattering image possible with what you have.

27

PATTERNS WITH SPECIAL FITTING FEATURES

With the aid of a few special pattern features, the fitting process can become even easier. The pattern companies want your sewing experiences to be as rewarding as possible, and that involves a positive, easy approach to all your fitting needs.

Certain Vogue Patterns include special fitting instructions. If the specific feature is valuable to you, look for it when you are selecting your patterns.

□ *Petite proportioned patterns:* include special adjustment lines for the Misses Petite figure type.

□ *Multi-size patterns:* include cutting lines for a range of sizes. If your bodice size differs from your skirt size, these patterns may save you the trouble of adjusting. Instructions for combining sizes are included on the pattern tissues.

Prepare to Fit

An organized approach is absolutely necessary in order to keep the fitting process simple, trouble free, and accurate. You are about to analyze, evaluate, and execute, all of which require a clear head and proper equipment.

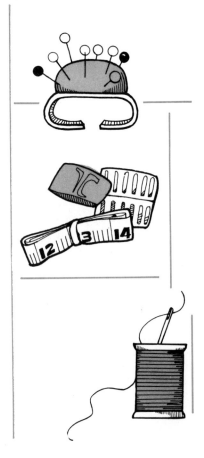

The space

The space you use for fitting should be a well-lighted section of your home, free from clutter and distractions. You need to be able to focus on your garment, not the surroundings. Soft, natural colors around you will contribute to the comfortable atmosphere.

The equipment

You will need a few basic pieces of equipment and some sewing tools—most of which you probably already have. The following list will help you organize your equipment; use it as a checklist as you prepare to fit.

□ *Full-length mirror:* two are even better, positioned so that you can see your back without twisting.

□ *Table:* to keep your tools close at hand.

□ *Iron and ironing board:* often necessary for a quick touch-up while fitting.

□ *Hanging space and padded hanger:* many times it's easier to work on your garment while it is hanging, so that you are able to move freely around the garment. A clothes tree works well . . . or a dress form, if you have one, is perfect for this.

□ *Sewing machine:* threaded and ready to go for alterations on the spot.

□ *Rulers:* a 6" (15cm) ruler with a sliding indicator is best for small changes; an 18" (46cm) see-through ruler is invaluable for flat pattern work.

□ *Tape measure:* the most accurate are made of nonstretch fibers; those printed on both sides are handy.

□ *Yardstick:* used to check grain lines, mark hems, and blend seamlines when making pattern changes.

□ *French curve:* used to draw curved lines for necklines, armholes, and seams; made of see-through plastic and shaped like a large J.

□ *T-square:* shaped like a T and used to determine cross grains and to alter patterns; an L-square can also be used.

□ *Pins:* necessary for fitting the garment; any rust-free dressmaker's pins will do.

□ *Pincushion:* a wrist type is perfect for fitting.

□ *Tissue paper:* essential for pattern adjustments; used for lengthening and filling in adjusted garment areas on the pattern pieces.

□ *Tape:* used to make pattern changes permanent; any type that can be marked on will do.

□ *Marking pens:* excellent for making final notations on pattern pieces; use washable pens and avoid those that smudge or bleed through the pattern tissue.

□ *Tracing paper and tracing wheel:* used to transfer markings from pattern to fabric.

□ *Tailor's chalk or marking pencil:* used for transferring pattern markings and for marking any needed fitting changes.

□ *Needle and thread:* needed for thread tracing and basting.

□ *Dressmaking shears:* those with 7" to 9" (18cm to 23cm) blades and an angled handle are best.

□ *Trimming scissors:* with 5" to 6" (12.6cm to 15cm) blades; used for clipping areas that need to be released while fitting.

□ *Seam ripper:* great for releasing basting during a fitting.

□ *Dress form:* can be exceedingly helpful but not necessary; if you already have one hidden in a closet, now is the time to get it out and put it to use. Be sure to adjust it according to your current measurements.

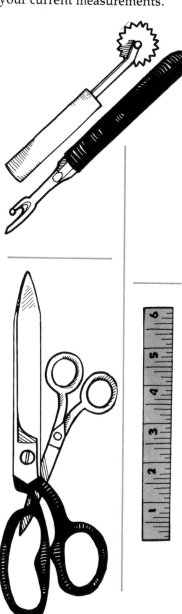

29

Taking Your Measurements

A custom fit begins with accurate measurements. Your final product can be only as accurate as the measurements you take, for they are the foundation upon which your fashion garment is made.

For the most reliable results, stand naturally and wear undergarments that support and distribute your weight in a manner that pleases you. Never measure over any clothing other than underwear or a body suit. Your shoes should be comfortable, with the heel height that you most commonly wear. It's easier to have someone help you with your measurements, but you can do it yourself with the help of a full-length mirror.

The basic measurements—bust, high bust, waist, hips, back waist length, and height—are necessary for selecting a pattern size. The other measurements will aid you in making pattern adjustments, so take them all carefully and accurately and record them for future use. Keep your chart handy at all times for adjustment and alteration comparisons.

If your weight tends to fluctuate or if you have a dramatic weight gain or loss, take your measurements again and record any changes.

Hold the tape measure tautly but not tightly against your body. Be certain the tape is always parallel to the floor for circumference measurements. Follow the directions below for each specific measurement; work with precision as you proceed with the first step toward a custom fit.

Before starting, tie a string around your waist and let it roll to the natural waistline. It should be snug, but not tight. Leave it there as a guide throughout the measuring process.

Evaluating Your Measurements

Having taken your measurements, you must now be able to evaluate and use them effectively as you select a proper figure type and pattern size. This information will also become essential for determining whether or not you need to make a fitting shell; if not, it will show what adjustments are necessary for each specific pattern you make, and whether a special test garment is necessary for a particular design. So the measurements will tell you much about your body and your needs as they relate to each sewing project you encounter.

Because women vary in size and shape, average figure types of varying proportions are the basis for the sizing of patterns. Standard body measurements have been established by the pattern industry for uniform sizing among all the companies. Thus you have a range of figure types and pattern sizes from which to choose. This is probably the single most important decision you will make in arriving at a good fit, so evaluate your measurements and select your figure type and pattern size carefully.

YOUR COMPLETE MEASUREMENTS

Bust Measure over the fullest part of the bust and then straight across the back(1).

High bust Measure around the body, directly under the arms and across the top of breasts (2).

Waist Measure circumference at the string (3).

High hip Measure circumference 2″ to 4″ (5cm to 10cm) below your waist over top of hip bones (4).

Full hip Measure circumference at fullest part of hips, mark position with pins on undergarments and measure down from waist over top of hip bones to pins, usually 7″ to 9″ (18cm to 23cm) down from the waist (5).

Back waist length Measure from prominent neck bone down center back to waistline (6).

Back width Measure from prominent neck bone down center back 4″ to 6″ (10cm to 15cm) and mark. Then measure at this point from arm crease to arm crease (7).

From neck to waist Measure from hollow between neck bones to center front waistline (8).

Bust point To establish position of bust point, measure from base of neck to bust point, and from bust point to center front at waist. Record both measurements (9).

Shoulder Measure from base of neck to shoulder bone (hinge) (10).

Arm length With arm slightly bent, measure from shoulder bone to elbow and on to wrist bone. Record both lengths (11).

Arm circumference Measure around fullest part of arm, generally 1″ (25mm) below armpit, and around wrist at bone (12,13).

Neck circumference Measure fullest part of neck (14).

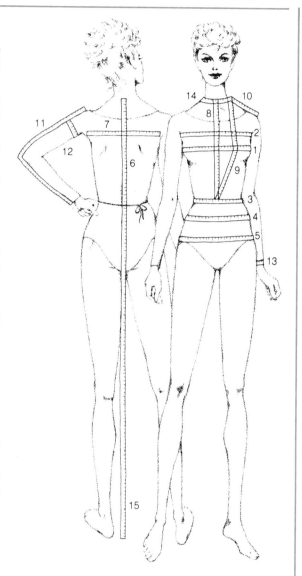

Skirt length Measure from center back waist to desired point on leg for hem (15).

Dress, jacket, blouse or vest length Measure from prominent neck bone to desired point on torso for hem (15).

Note: Refer to p. 166 for information on taking pants measurements.

FIGURE TYPES

Figure type is a matter of proportion, not age. The overall proportion of your body—the length of your torso, the location of your bust and hips in relation to your waist, and the difference between your bust, waist, and hip measurements—is the most important factor in determining your figure type.

To evaluate the length of your torso, compare your back waist length and height with those measurements for each figure type. Measure the distance from your waistline to your hips to determine the proportions of your figure. The measurements of your bust, waist, and hips will indicate their relative circumference proportions.

To determine your figure type, compare your bust, waist, hip, back waist, length and height measurements with those on the measurement charts in any pattern catalog. You will probably find that your measurements will not match up exactly to any one type. This is most common; you will choose the figure type whose measurements most closely match your own.

If, in comparing your measurements, you find that you fall between figure types, it's time to make a critical analysis of your body structure: is your body long and slender or shorter and more closely proportioned? Refer to the descriptions of each figure type and use your good sense as you decide which is closest to yours.

Measurement Chart, Misses' Size

Body Measurements *in inches (and centimeters)*

SIZE	6	8	10	12	14	16	18	20	22
Bust	30½(78)	31½(80)	32½(83)	34(87)	36(92)	38(97)	40(102)	42(107)	44(112)
Waist	23(58)	24(61)	25(64)	26½(67)	28(71)	30(76)	32(81)	34(87)	36(92)
Hip	32½(83)	33½(85)	34½(88)	36(92)	38(97)	40(102)	42(107)	44(112)	46(117)
Back Waist Length	15½(39.5)	15¾(40)	16(40.5)	16¼(41.5)	16½(42)	16¾(42.5)	17(43)	17¼(44)	17½(44.5)

Misses' Petite

SIZE	6	8	10	12	14	16	18
Bust	30½(78)	31½(80)	32½(83)	34(87)	36(92)	38(97)	40(102)
Waist	23½(60)	24½(60)	25½(65)	27(69)	28½(73)	30½(78)	32½(83)
Hip	32½(83)	33½(85)	34½(88)	36(92)	38(97)	40(102)	42(107)
Back Waist Length	14½(37)	14¾(37.5)	15(38)	15¼(39)	15½(39.5)	15¾(40)	16(40.5)

PATTERN SIZE

After you have determined your figure type you are ready to choose a pattern size. Use the measurement chart on page 32 or the measurement charts in the pattern catalog to find the size that most closely matches your bust, waist, and hips.

The measurements listed on the chart are actual body measurements. The tissue patterns have extra ease called "wearing ease" built in beyond the actual body measurements to give you room to move in your garment. Many patterns have additional ease, called "design ease," built in to create a certain silhouette. Always choose your pattern size by comparing your measurements to the body measurements listed on the chart, not to the actual pattern measurements.

If your measurements do not

Flattering images can be created
by choosing designs that compliment your figure.
The elements of each design should
contribute to an appearance
that is pleasing and flattering. Learn to use design
elements to your best advantage.

*Two-piece designs of a single color
tend to create a longer, slimmer image
while contrasting colors shorten the
body proportions and sometimes add
width to the overall image.*

*Vertical lines lengthen and slim the
body proportions; horizontal lines
create a shorter and wider image.*

Small prints tend to recede making the figure appear small; large prints tend to advance making the figure appear larger.

The position of the horizontal seams such as a waistline seam in a design can create different illusions on a particular figure. Well-proportioned figures can wear waistline seams at the natural waistline. Figures that are short-waisted or long-waisted may find a high or low waist seam more flattering.

Dark colors tend to recede, a more flattering image on a larger figure; light and bright colors tend to advance, making a figure appear larger.

A figure with narrow or sloping shoulders can broaden the look with fashions that have design accents or horizontal emphasis at the shoulder, full puffed sleeves, or exaggerated shoulder lines.

Figures with broad or square shoulders can soften the image with designs including shoulder lines that fall off the shoulder or designs with a raglan or kimono sleeve.

Small-busted figures can create a more flattering illusion by adding fullness at the bust area with design features such as ruffles, pockets, and horizontal lines. Designs with proportionately larger bodices and slimmer skirts can also add an illusion of fullness to a small bustline.

Simple, longer lines and accents away from the bust area are the best choices for a large bustline. Designs that fall softly over the bust without clinging to it will always create a more flattering image for this figure.

Figures with a full waist will be most flattered in designs without a fitted waistline. Pants covered with a long sweater or tunic, dresses with a raised or dropped waistline, and long slim no-waistline designs will create the image you want.

Heavy hips and thighs can be dressed to project balanced and flattering proportions with soft fabrics and a gentle fullness. Vertical lines will tend to slim the figure, and pants that are semifitted with soft pleats and straight legs are the best choice.

A body with narrow hips can broaden the image to create a more balanced illusion by choosing designs with horizontal lines below the waistline. Full gathered skirts and heavily textured fabrics will also add width to the hip area.

To create an image of slimness, choose designs with vertical lines, long proportions, soft or dark colors, and slim silhouettes.

To create an image of fullness, choose designs with layers of fabric, horizontal lines, short proportions, bold or bright colors, and full silhouettes.

correspond exactly to any one size, consider all the pertinent factors and choose the size requiring the fewest major adjustments. The following suggestions will help you select the best size for you.

☐ Your pattern size probably will not be the same as your ready-to-wear size. Do not use your ready-to-wear size as a guideline; instead, rely on your measurements.

☐ Dress, blouse, top, vest, coat, and jacket sizes should be selected according to your bust measurement. If there is a difference of more than 2″ (5cm) between your bust and high bust measurements, this is an indication that you have a fuller bust in relation to your body frame than the standard pattern measurements. Since patterns are designed for a B cup bust, you will achieve a better fit through your shoulders, chest, and upper back if you select a pattern size by your high bust measurement and alter the bust area as necessary. If your waist and hips do not correspond to the measurements for this pattern size they can be easily adjusted; it is easier to make the adjustments in either or both of these areas than to alter the bodice.

☐ Skirt, pants, shorts or culotte patterns should be selected by the waist measurement. If your hips are proportionally much larger than your waist, select the size closest to your hip

measurement and adjust the waist.

☐ When purchasing a coordinate pattern that includes a blouse, skirt, jacket, and pants, select your size by your bust or high bust measurement and adjust the waist and hips if necessary.

☐ If your measurements fall between sizes, consider factors such as bone structure, fabric, pattern design, and personal preference. The smaller size may be better if you are small boned, the larger if you are large boned. Some fabrics offer more give than others, allowing you to choose the smaller size; with heavy, thick, or firm fabrics you may want the larger size. A pattern style that is loose or very loose fitting can usually be purchased in the smaller size; one that is fitted or semi-fitted should be purchased in the larger size. Personal preference will certainly have a strong influence on your selection; you may be inclined toward a closer or looser fit. Follow these guidelines and your instincts when you fall between sizes.

☐ Maternity patterns should be purchased in the same size that you wore before your pregnancy.

UNDERSTANDING EASE

Ease is the additional fullness built into a garment beyond the actual body measurements. The amount of ease in each

fashion is determined by both function and style.

A limited amount of ease is necessary to make the garment comfortable to wear and useful for its purpose. A blouse intended to be worn next to the body needs much less ease than a jacket that is intended to be worn over a blouse and/or possibly a sweater. This ease, commonly called wearing ease, provides built-in livability and allows for freedom of movement without restraint. Never use wearing ease to accommodate a larger size or eliminate it when making pattern adjustments and alterations.

Some patterns have little or no wearing ease; these are limited to special designs such as strapless and halter-neck bodices and garments with cutaway armholes. Evening wear, swimwear, and sportswear made of stretch fabrics as well as any other patterns designed especially for stretchable knits normally have less than the standard amounts of wearing ease; they rely on the give of the fabric to provide the necessary room for movement.

The additional fullness added to a garment to create a specific silhouette is design ease. The amount of design ease built into a garment varies with the style as well as with fashion trends. The caption on the pattern envelope gives the first indication of how much design ease has been added to that design.

A closely fitted garment would have no design ease and little or no wearing ease. A fitted garment would have little or no design ease but would include the standard amounts of wearing ease. A semi-fitted garment may have up to 4" (10cm) of ease in the bust, a loosely fitted garment up to 8" (20.5cm), and a very loosely fitted garment over 8" (20.5cm). The following chart includes the design ease allowances for different types of garments.

The pattern description in the catalogue and on the back of the pattern envelope will indicate how each garment is intended to fit. The chart on page 35 defines the amount of ease given for each silhouette. Use this information to help give you a clear picture of each garment's fit and shape.

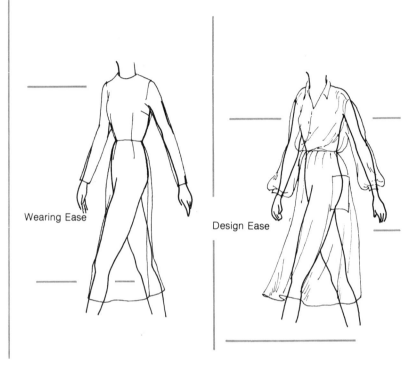

Wearing Ease

Design Ease

Ease Allowance Chart
(Includes Both Wearing and Design Ease)

SILHOUETTES	BUST AREA			HIP AREA
	DRESSES, BLOUSES SHIRTS, TOPS, VESTS	JACKETS Lined or Unlined	COATS Lined or Unlined	SKIRTS, PANTS SHORTS, CULOTTES
Close fitting	0"-2⅞" (0cm-7.3cm)	NOT APPLICABLE	NOT APPLICABLE	NOT APPLICABLE
Fitted	3"-4" (7.5cm-10cm)	3¾"-4¼" (9.5cm-10.7cm)	5¼"-6¾" (13.3cm-17cm)	2"-3" (5cm-7.5cm)
Semi-fitted	4⅛"-5" (10.4cm-12.5cm)	4⅜"-5¾" (11.1cm-14.5cm)	6⅞"-8" (17.4cm-20.5cm)	3⅛"-4" (7.9cm-10cm)
Loose fitting	5⅛"-8" (13cm-20.5cm)	5⅞"-10" (14.8cm-25.5cm)	8⅛"-12" (20.7cm-30.5cm)	4⅛"-6" (10.4cm-15cm)
Very loose fitting	Over 8" (over 20.5cm)	Over 10" (over 25.5cm)	Over 12" (over 30.5cm)	Over 6" (over 15cm)

Comparing Measurements

In order to determine if any tissue pattern adjustments must be made, compare your body measurements to the standard body measurements for your size. The difference will indicate how much of an adjustment is necessary at each position. The chart below includes the standard body measurements of eight crucial positions for each pattern size. Use it as you proceed with the first step of adjusting your pattern.

After having taken your body measurements for each of these positions (p. 31), chart the standard body measurements for your size next to them and determine the difference. Make a list of each adjustment necessary to bring your pattern into proportion with your body.

If you are making a fitting shell or a fitted design, adjust your pattern the exact amount of the difference at each position. Fitted silhouettes are designed close to the body and

include only the minimum amounts of ease necessary for comfort.

With loose-fitting silhouettes, you must be able to analyse the design and decide if an adjustment is necessary. For instance, if your shoulder is ¼" (6mm) broader than the standard, and you are making a loose-fitted garment with a kimono sleeve, a shoulder adjustment would be a useless exercise. On the other hand, suppose you are making a gar-

Standard Body Measurements
Measurements are given in inches (centimeters)

SIZE	6	8	10	12	14	16	18	20	22
Bust	30½	31½	32½	34	36	38	40	42	44
	(78)	(80)	(83)	(87)	(92)	(97)	(102)	(107)	(112)
Waist	23	24	25	26½	28	30	32	34	36
	(58)	(61)	(64)	(67)	(71)	(76)	(81)	(87)	(92)
Hip	32½	33½	34½	36	38	40	42	44	46
	(83)	(85)	(88)	(92)	(97)	(102)	(107)	(112)	(117)
Back Waist Length	15½	15¾	16	16¼	16½	16¾	17	17¼	17½
	(39.5)	(40)	(40.5)	(41.5)	(42)	(42.5)	(43)	(44)	(44.5)
Back Width (4" [10cm] below base of neck)	13¼	13⅝	14	14½	15	15½	16	16½	17
	(33.5)	(34.5)	(35.5)	(37)	(38)	(39.5)	(40.5)	(42)	(43)
Sleeve Length (Shoulder to Wrist)	21¼	21⅝	21⅞	22¼	22½	22⅞	23¼	23½	23⅞
	(54)	(55)	(55.5)	(56.5)	(57)	(58)	(59)	(59.5)	(60.5)
Arm Circumference (1" [25mm] below armpit)	9⅜	9⅝	10	10⅜	10⅞	11½	12⅛	12¾	13⅜
	(23.8)	(24.5)	(25.5)	(26.3)	(27.6)	(29.2)	(30.5)	(32.5)	(34)
Skirt/Dress Length (Waistline to Mid-knee)	22¾	22¾	22¾	22¾	22¾	22¾	22¾	22¾	22¾
	(58)	(58)	(58)	(58)	(58)	(58)	(58)	(58)	(58)

ment that is semi-fitted and your hips measure 2″ (5cm) larger than the standard for your size. Refer to the ease allowance chart (p. 34) and you will see that the hip area on a semi-fitted design has 3⅛″ to 4″ (7.9cm to 10cm) of ease. In this case it would be necessary to make an adjustment in order to preserve the intended design of the garment.

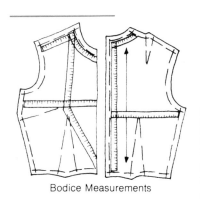

Bodice Measurements

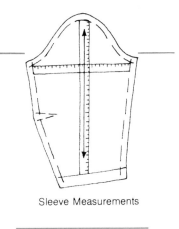

Sleeve Measurements

Personal Measurement Worksheet

Use this chart as a permanent record of fitting changes you'll need to make. Enter your measurements in the first column. Refer to the chart on the previous page for the standard body measurements that correspond to the pattern size you customarily purchase and enter these in the second column. Be sure to list the pattern size here also. Use the last column to record any differences, plus or minus, that you'll need to make to achieve a perfect fit.

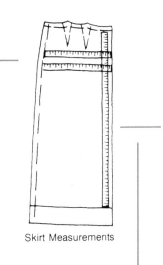

Skirt Measurements

	Personal body measurements	Pattern size _____ Standard body measurements	Difference (+ or −)
Bust	_____	_____	_____
Waist	_____	_____	_____
Hip	_____	_____	_____
Back Waist Length	_____	_____	_____
Back Width	_____	_____	_____
Sleeve Length	_____	_____	_____
Arm Circumference	_____	_____	_____
Skirt/Dress Length	_____	_____	_____

3 Pattern Tissue Adjustments

Understanding the fundamentals of pattern tissue adjustments can be the beginning of a whole wardrobe of personalized fashions. Simple length and/or circumference adjustments may be all you need to create garments that flatter you and your individual proportions.

Now that you know the variations between your own and the standard body measurements on which the patterns have been based, you can make the particular adjustments necessary for each item you choose to sew.

Pattern tissue adjustments are neither difficult nor time consuming once you understand the procedure—and you need to understand only the ones you will require. So, decide which adjustments you need to make and proceed, using this chapter as an encyclopedia and referring only to those which apply to you.

Prepare to Adjust

WHERE TO START

You will be able to determine which adjustments you need by comparing your measurements to the standard body measurements for your size (page 35). You probably also have some experience with ill-fitting garments that you have made or purchased before. If the waistlines typically fall above your natural waistline, it is a good indication you need a lengthening adjustment; if your skirts are typically snug at the hipline, it is a good indication that the hipline is falling at the wrong place (a length adjustment) or that the width of the skirt is inadequate (a circumference adjustment). Proper measurements compared to the standard pattern measurements will help you determine which adjustment is needed.

DOING IT RIGHT

Accuracy is extremely important when making adjustments. You must proceed logically and carefully each step of the way. An error in measuring, corresponding pattern pieces missing an adjustment, or seamlines that don't match can lead to fitting errors.

The step-by-step procedures outlined on the following pages will guide you through each adjustment with ease. You will soon learn the fundamentals involved in perfecting your fit efficiently and accurately.

THE STEP BEYOND

If you find the basic length and circumference adjustments are not enough to achieve a satisfactory fit for your proportions, you may need to make one or perhaps several of the alterations described in Chapter 5 for specific figure characteristics.

It may be helpful to make a fitting shell to determine all the alterations you might need; Chapter 4 provides these instructions.

If you already have a good concept of the specific adjustments and alterations you need, you can go ahead and apply them to your fashion pattern. For example, if your garments typically drag at the shoulder and you recognize that you have a sloped shoulder, you may not find it necessary to make a fitting shell. You can simply refer to the directions for a sloped shoulder adjustment and apply it to your fashion pattern.

ADJUST WITH ACCURACY

The more you understand your body and its individuality, the easier it will be to decide what pattern adjustments are necessary for a flattering fit. There are no secrets or mysteries to pattern tissue adjustments; they are simply the first adjustments you will make and they are done while the pattern tissue and fabric are flat. When you have completed your adjustments, the pattern tissue must still remain flat.

Ideally, the more accurate and complete you are with your pattern tissue adjustments, the fewer alterations you will have to make on your completed garment. As you develop your skills and learn to analyze your individual adjustment needs more exactly, it will be easier for you to make most of your adjustment decisions at this point in the construction process.

Always complete all the necessary adjustments on the pattern tissue before cutting any fabric. It is important that you double-check each adjustment for accuracy before you proceed.

Keep these rules in mind when making any pattern tissue adjustments:

□ Press all pattern pieces with a warm dry iron before you attempt any adjustments.

□ Make only the adjustments necessary for a good fit.

□ Maintain the original design lines of the garment.

□ Maintain the wearing ease designed into the garment.

□ Use the adjustment lines provided for lengthening and shortening.

□ Mark and pin the adjustment first, check it with a tape measure for accuracy, and then tape it carefully in place.

□ Follow a logical order: Make all length adjustments first, then adjust circumference. Finally, make any special adjustments necessary for a personalized fit.

□ Make necessary changes on all corresponding pattern pieces. For example, if you lengthen the bodice front, you must do the same to the bodice back. If you make any changes at the neckline, you must adjust any facings, bands, or collars accordingly (A).

A

□ Keep grainlines straight at the completion of the adjustment. Note the grainline on the original piece and make certain you preserve it on the altered piece.

□ Make certain pattern pieces are flat when the adjustment is completed.

□ Redraw any cutting and construction lines that have been interrupted by the adjustments. Simply join the two ends and create a new line. To reestablish a smooth straight line, place a ruler along the two original lines and taper to join. With curved lines, redraw freehand or use a French curve to create a smooth, even line.

□ Correct any markings on the pattern pieces that may have been affected by the adjustment. For example, length adjustments would require respacing the buttonhole markings, and certain length and circumference adjustments would necessitate changes in pocket placement. Other markings that may be affected would be trims, zipper placement, casings, darts, and bands. It's a good idea to make a quick check of all pattern markings to determine if they were affected by the adjustments.

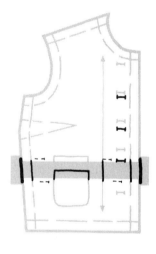

□ Double-check all completed adjustments for accuracy. Check grainlines, corresponding pieces, and all pattern markings. It is helpful to match the notches on the pattern tissue to see that all joining seamlines will still meet accurately. Check to be sure that all interrupted lines have been corrected and that the pattern lies flat (B).

B

□ Adjust your fabric purchase accordingly. Any substantial adjustments may require more or less fabric than the pattern envelope suggests. The pattern company has allowed adequate yardage requirements for any minor adjustments, but you may have to buy a different amount if your adjustments are substantial.

Length Adjustments

When analyzing your measurements to determine needed adjustments you may find an interesting combination of statistics. You may be long waisted with a shorter than average hipline, or your arm may be longer from shoulder to elbow and average from elbow to wrist; thus you must adjust the pattern lengths to your personal needs. Shortening or lengthening your pattern pieces is an easy adjustment to make and is crucial to correcting many fitting problems.

You will find adjustment lines on all major pattern pieces: bodice front and back, skirt front and back, and sleeves. You will also find adjustment lines on corresponding pattern pieces such as center front bands, fly front extensions, pleat inserts, and any other pieces that are attached to the major pieces.

Some pattern pieces will indicate an adjustment at the lower edge of the tissue.

Redraw interrupted lines to retain smooth, even construction lines. Use a felt-tip pen or a soft lead pencil so you can mark new lines clearly without tearing the tissue. Merely connecting the original lines will not do—you must add to one interrupted line and subtract from the other, re-establishing the smooth contours of your pattern's cutting and stitching lines. Taper the new lines to the original ones and connect interrupted

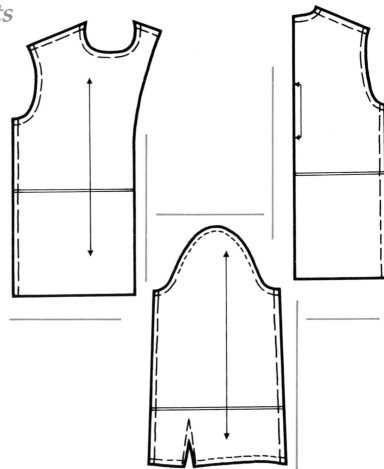

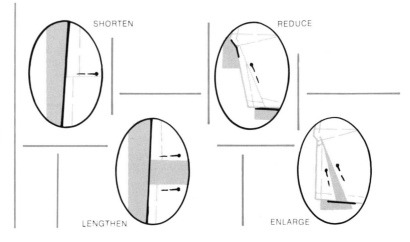

SHORTEN

REDUCE

LENGTHEN

ENLARGE

grainlines. In some cases it may be necessary to extend the pattern edges with tissue paper to redraw the cutting lines.

Remember to make the same adjustments on all corresponding pattern pieces such as facings, bands, and pleat inserts. *Note:* throughout Chapters 3-6 wherever pattern pieces are illustrated, only front pattern pieces are shown. Equal changes must be made on front, back and other re- lated pieces like facings, waistbands, etc. On the pattern pieces, bold lines indicate corrected cutting and dart lines.

SHORTENING PATTERN PIECES

Determine the amount needed to shorten and measure down from the adjustment line carefully at two points. Place a ruler on the tissue joining the two points and draw a line parallel to the adjustment line. Fold the pattern on the printed adjustment line and place the fold along the newly drawn line. Pin or tape in place.

Correct any interrupted cutting lines, seamlines, darts, and other markings.

To shorten along the lower edge of skirts, jackets, etc., measure and mark the change, then cut away the excess. A curved ruler is helpful when marking a shaped hemline edge. Simply match the curve of the ruler to the printed edge and move the ruler to the new markings to draw a parallel line. It is important to maintain a similar curve along the new line.

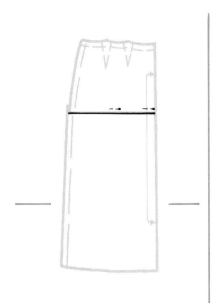

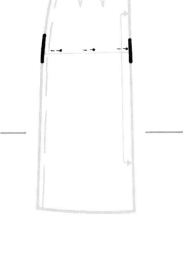

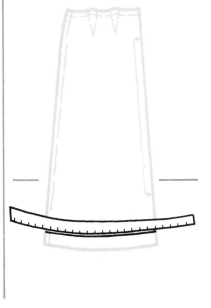

Patterns with adjustment features for the Misses Petite figure type, called Petite Proportioned patterns, would be done in the same manner. Basically, these patterns will have additional adjustment lines in areas such as the upper chest, the upper arm, and between the waistline and hipline. If you are using a pattern with instructions for the Misses Petite figure, watch for these additional adjustment lines.

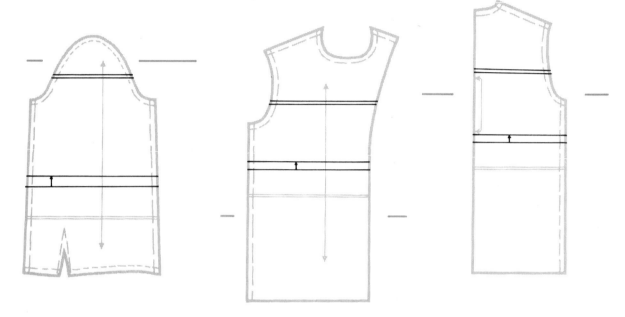

Unfitted skirts

Unfitted designs such as the circular or gathered skirt are shortened along the lower edge. No hipline adjustment is necessary in unfitted designs.

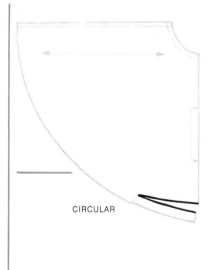

CIRCULAR

Fitted skirts

Fitted skirt patterns and any variations such as the gored skirt are adjusted in two positions. To raise the hip, adjust below the waistline; to shorten the finished length, cut away from the lower edge.

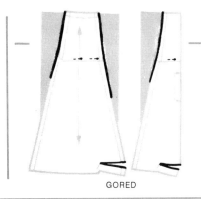

GORED

Fitted dresses

For a shorter waist, eliminate length on the bodice front and back along the adjustment lines provided. To raise the hip, shorten the skirt pattern along the adjustment line below the waistline. Remove any additional unnecessary length along the lower edge. Make the same adjustments on all corresponding pieces such as facings, bands, and pleat inserts. Blouses, jackets, coats, and vests are shortened in the same manner.

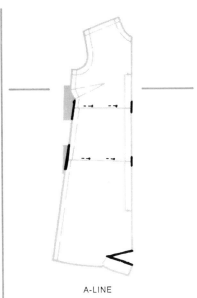

A-LINE

A-line dresses

To raise the waist, shorten above the waistline; to raise the hip, shorten below the waistline. Additional length can be eliminated at the lower edge, if necessary. Adjust the dress back and any corresponding pieces such as facings, bands, and pleat inserts at the same places. Coat patterns with an A-line design would be adjusted in the same manner.

FITTED

Princess dresses

To raise the waist, shorten above the waistline; to raise the hip, shorten below the waistline. Any additional length can be removed along the lower edge. Princess designs have two bodice fronts and two bodice backs. Adjust all pieces and any corresponding pieces such as bands, facings, and pleat inserts at the same places. Coat patterns with a princess design are adjusted in the same manner.

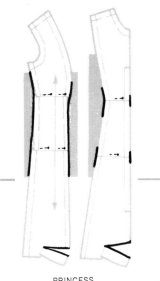

PRINCESS

43

Unfitted sleeves

Unfitted sleeves such as shirt, raglan and kimono sleeves have only one adjustment line. Shorten the full amount necessary at the line provided.

Fitted sleeves

Fitted sleeves, with an elbow dart or ease, will have two adjustment lines, one above the elbow and one below. Compare your measurements to the pattern and shorten the sleeve where necessary.

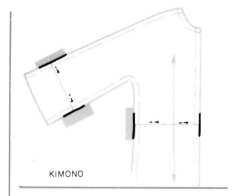

KIMONO

RAGLAN

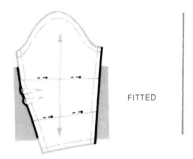

FITTED

LENGTHENING PATTERN PIECES

The same adjustment lines used for shortening a pattern are also used for lengthening. Determine the amount you need to lengthen, cut the pattern along the adjustment line, and pin or tape a strip of tissue paper to the upper section of the pattern piece. Measure and mark the adjustment at two

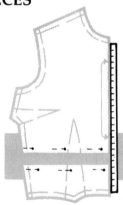

points, and use a ruler to draw a line joining the points parallel to the printed adjustment line. Carefully place the bottom section of the pattern tissue along the drawn line and pin or tape it to the tissue.

Place a ruler along the grainline or center fold line to help you position the unat-

tached section properly. It's important that grainlines are joined evenly.

Correct any interrupted cutting lines, seamlines, darts, and other markings. Adjust all corresponding pattern pieces and remember to determine if any additional fabric will be required.

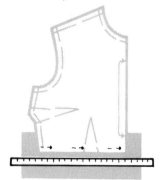

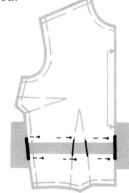

To lengthen along a lower edge of a pattern piece, pin or tape tissue paper along the lower edge; then measure and mark the adjustment carefully. A curved ruler is helpful when lengthening pieces with a curved edge, just as when shortening. Match the curve of the ruler to the printed line, move the ruler to the new markings, and draw a line parallel to the original.

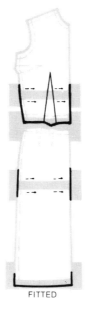

Fitted dresses

For a longer waist, add length to the bodice front and back at the adjustment lines provided. To lower the hip, add length along the adjustment line below the waistline. Any additional length needed should be added along the lower edge. Make the same adjustments on all corresponding pieces such as facings, bands, and pleat inserts. Blouses, jack-ets, coats, and vests are lengthened in the same manner.

FITTED

A-line dresses

To lower the waist, add length above the waistline; to lower the hip, add length below the waistline. Additional length can be added at the lower edge if needed. Adjust the dress back and any corresponding pieces such as facings, bands, and pleat inserts at the same places. Coat patterns with an A-line design would be adjusted in the same manner.

Princess dresses

To lower the waist, lengthen above the waistline; to lower the hip, lengthen below the waistline. Any additional length needed can be added along the lower edge. Princess designs have two bodice fronts and two bodice backs. Adjust all pieces and any corresponding pieces at the same places. Coat patterns with a princess design would be adjusted in the same manner.

A-LINE

PRINCESS

Fitted skirts

Fitted skirt patterns and any variations such as the gored skirt are adjusted in two positions. To lower the hip, adjust below the waistline; to provide additional length, add to the lower edge.

Unfitted skirts

Unfitted designs such as the circular or gathered skirt are lengthened along the lower edge. No hipline adjustment is necessary in unfitted designs.

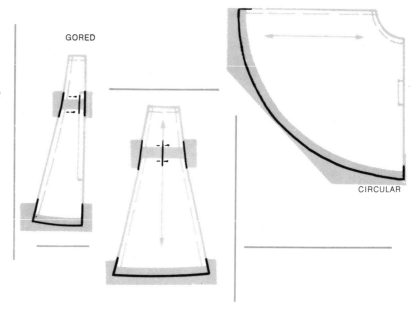

GORED

CIRCULAR

Fitted sleeves

Fitted sleeves with an elbow dart or ease will have two adjustment lines, one above the elbow and one below. Compare your measurements to the pattern and lengthen the sleeve where necessary.

Unfitted sleeves

Unfitted sleeves such as shirt, raglan and kimono sleeves have only one adjustment line. Lengthen the full amount needed at the line provided.

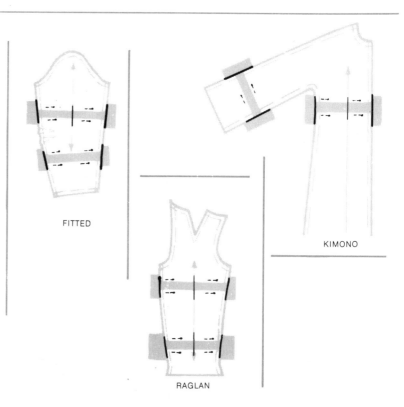

FITTED

KIMONO

RAGLAN

SPECIAL SITUATIONS

Combining adjustments

When several adjustments have to be made, the length adjustments are always done first. Start with those above the waist and
then do those below the waist. You may have to shorten the pattern in one area and lengthen it in another in order to match the
proportions of your own body. Proceed with any circumference
adjustments next and all specialized adjustments last.

Intricate pattern pieces

Many times a pattern will have
unusual seaming, making a
simple adjustment appear complicated. Don't despair!
Analyze the pattern pieces to
determine where the adjustment lines should fall, and you
will find them clearly marked
on each section.
  On some pattern pieces such
as those with French darts, the
adjustment line could be in
several sections of the pattern
at unusual angles because of
the seaming. Adjust each section along the adjustment
lines, as necessary.

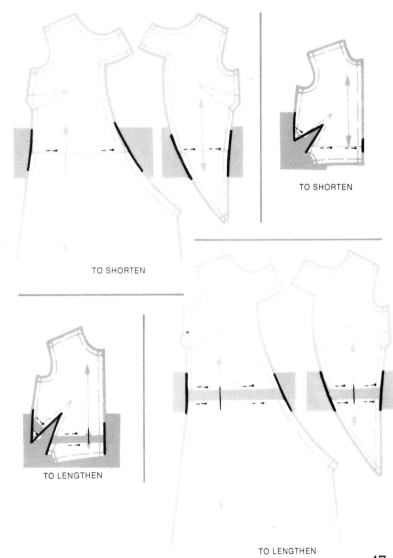

TO SHORTEN

TO SHORTEN

TO LENGTHEN

TO LENGTHEN

47

Uneven adjustments

In situations where the back waist length is shorter or longer than the front waist length, it will be necessary to make an uneven adjustment on fitted or semi-fitted garments. Make the necessary adjustment at the adjustment line above the waistline on the bodice back.

To lengthen the back, slash the pattern from the center back to the side seam. Spread the pattern the necessary amount at the center back, tapering to nothing at the side seam. Redraw the grainline, seamlines, and cutting lines by extending the original lines from the bodice. Extend the hemline or waistline seam along the original line. Correct any affected darts by tapering from the base to the point.

To shorten the back, mark the adjustment at the center back and fold out the excess length, tapering to nothing at the side seam. It may be necessary to clip the pattern slightly at the side seam allowance so that it will lie smoothly. Redraw the grainline, seamlines, and cutting lines by extending the original lines from the bodice. Extend the hemline or waistline seam along the original line. Correct any affected darts by tapering from the base to the point.

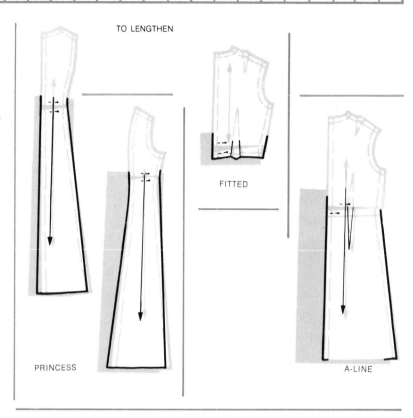

TO LENGTHEN

PRINCESS

FITTED

A-LINE

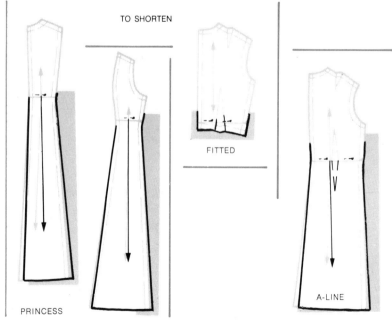

TO SHORTEN

PRINCESS

FITTED

A-LINE

Circumference Adjustments

Changing the pattern to coincide with your body contours allows you to customize the fit of your garment. You will be delighted with the way your garment will actually flatter your figure when your own proportions are built into the pattern before you ever cut the fabric.

Circumference adjustments are used to increase or decrease the width of a pattern to accommodate your particular figure. You may find that your bust and hips are proportionately the same as the pattern, but your waist is smaller. On the other hand, you may find that your arms and thighs are proportionately larger than your pattern size. Circumference adjustments can make each garment fit as if it were specifically designed for you.

Small circumference adjustments are normally done at the side seams of bodice and skirt pieces and at the underarm seams of sleeves. If the adjustment needed is substantial, it is better to slash the pattern to avoid distorting the design. The following sections will explain when to adjust at seams and when it is necessary to slash the pattern.

Each major pattern piece, except the sleeve, represents one quarter of your body. Consequently, each bodice or skirt pattern piece must be increased or decreased one quarter of the total adjustment needed. For example, a required waistline adjustment of 1" (25mm) would be translated to the bodice front side seams as ¼" (6mm) and to the bodice back side seams as ¼" (6mm).

On pattern pieces representing the complete front or back of a garment, or those where the right side is different from the left side, you simply need to make a quarter of the total adjustment on both sides of the pattern piece.

To adjust the pattern at the side seams

Determine the amount of the total adjustment needed at each position (hip, waist, bust, etc.). Measure and mark one-fourth of the increase or decrease along the cutting line.

To get the correct angle of the seam allowance in the bust dart area, first pin the dart in place along the dart stitching line. Then with the dart shaped and seamlines in place, cut or mark the new cutting line. Remove the pins and you will have a correctly tapered seam allowance at the dart.

To adjust the pattern by slashing

To avoid distorting the design, any substantial adjustments should be done by slashing the pattern rather than by increasing or decreasing the side seams. Follow the specific instructions for each adjustment on the following pages.

It is important to have adequate tissue paper to place behind the pattern when increasing the circumference. Measure and pin carefully before you tape the tissue and always work on a large flat surface.

To reduce the circumference, slash the pattern as far as necessary so it will lie flat when you lap the edges the amount

to be decreased. Clip the seam allowance to the seamline, or clip the hem allowance to the hemline, so the pattern lies flat.

To enlarge the circumference, slash the pattern as far as necessary for the pattern to lie flat. Place tissue paper under the slashed edges and spread the amount needed. Form a pleat in the seam allowance or hem allowance so the pattern will lie flat.

Redraw interrupted lines to achieve smooth, even construction lines. Use a felt-tip pen or a soft lead pencil so you can mark new lines clearly

without tearing the tissue. Merely connecting the original lines will not do—you must add to one interrupted line and subtract from the other, re-establishing the smooth contours of your pattern's cutting and stitching lines. Taper the new lines to the original ones and connect interrupted grainlines. In some cases it may be necessary to extend the pattern edges with tissue paper to redraw the cutting lines.

Remember to make the same adjustments on all corresponding pattern pieces such as facings, waistbands, casings, and bands.

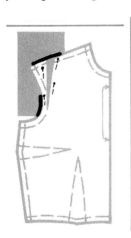

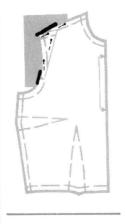

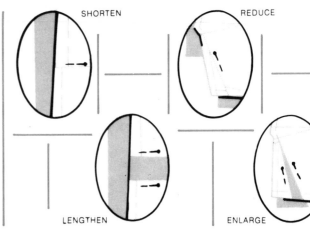

REDUCING THE WAIST

If you have a slender waistline yet proportionate bust and hips, garments will collapse at your waist giving an unkempt, haphazard look. It will therefore be necessary to reduce the waist without changing the hip circumference.

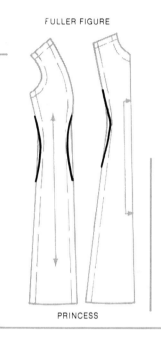

FULLER FIGURE

PRINCESS

A-line dresses

To reduce the waist of an A-line style, mark one-fourth of the amount needed at the waist indication. Draw new cutting lines, tapering from the waist to near the bust dart, and from the waist to just above the hipline. The line should not be tapered to the hipline, as doing so would reduce your pattern's hip measurement.

Princess dresses

To reduce the waist of a princess style garment, there are two advance considerations. If you have a full figure, you can safely reduce the waist at the side front and side back seams as well as at the side seams. Divide the amount of reduction by the number of seams; halve this number for the reduction to be made at each seam edge. Mark the amount and draw new cutting lines, tapering from the waist to just under the bust, and from the waist to just above the full hip, since you do not want to disturb the bust and hip proportions of your pattern.

Or, if you are on the small side, you can make waist reductions in a princess style only at the side seams. To do this, mark one-fourth of the amount needed at the waist indication. Draw in new cutting lines, tapering from the waist to just under the bust and from the waist to just above the full hip.

A-LINE

SMALLER FIGURE

NO CHANGE

PRINCESS

Fitted dresses

On the bodice and skirt side seams of a design with a waist seam, mark one-fourth of the amount needed to be reduced. Draw new cutting lines, tapering from the waist to just below the bust on the bodice, and from the waist to just above the hipline on the skirt; the hip circumference is not reduced.

Fitted skirts

On designs such as a gored skirt, make the waist reduction at the side seams for a smaller figure; mark ¼ of the amount needed. Draw new cutting lines, tapering from the waist to just above the hipline. For a fuller figure, divide the amount of change by the number of seams as explained for princess styles.

Unfitted skirts

For a circular skirt, place tissue paper above the waist edge and draw in a new waist seamline, reducing one-fourth of the amount needed; follow the curves of the pattern. Then draw new cutting lines and foldlines as indicated on these pattern pieces. On a semicircular skirt which has no hip shaping, the waist reduction is done in the same manner.

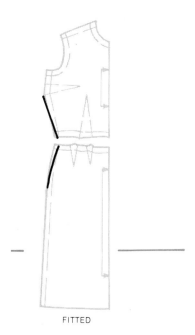

FITTED

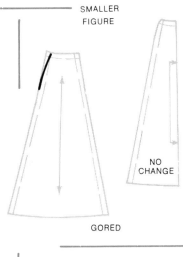

SMALLER
FIGURE

NO
CHANGE

GORED

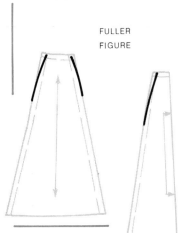

FULLER
FIGURE

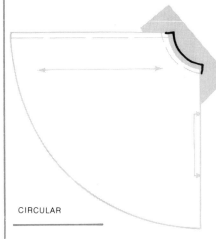

CIRCULAR

Waistband

Adjust a waistband to correspond to the skirt by reducing it the full amount needed. Add one-half of the amount of the change at the center front. Add the other half of this amount at the center back or at each side seam marking so all your symbols will match those on the skirt.

WAISTBAND

ENLARGING THE WAIST

The woman with a fuller waistline in proportion to her bust and hips is one of an endless variety of figure types. To avoid making this adjustment ruins the look of the garment and restricts comfort and movement. Do not use the built-in wearing ease to accommodate a larger waistline.

A-line dresses

For an A-line style, add tissue paper to the side seam. Mark one-fourth of the amount needed at the waist and draw new cutting lines; taper from the waist to just under the bust dart, and from the waist to just above the hipline. This prevents disturbing bust and hip measurements.

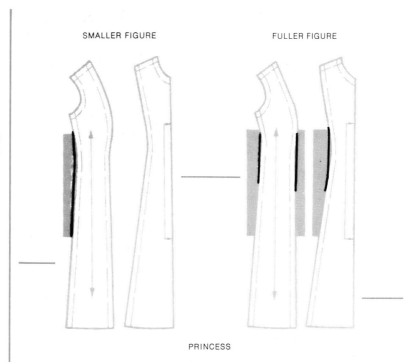

SMALLER FIGURE

FULLER FIGURE

PRINCESS

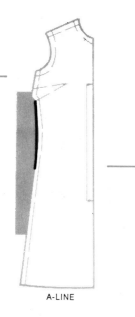

A-LINE

Princess dresses

To enlarge the waist of a princess style, take figure proportions into account. For a smaller figure, the waist may be enlarged at the side seams only. To do this, add tissue paper to the side seam. Mark one-fourth of the amount needed to be enlarged and draw in new cutting lines, tapering from the waist to just under the bust and from the waist to just above the full hip, so the hip and bust measurements of your pattern remain the same.

To make this adjustment for a fuller figure, divide the amount needed by the number of seams; halve this figure for the amount of change that will be needed at each seam edge. Do not add to center front or back seams. Then increase the waist as previously explained.

Fitted dresses

To a design with a waist seam, add tissue paper to the side seams of the bodice and skirt. Mark one-fourth of the amount needed to be enlarged at the waistline. Draw new cutting lines, tapering from the waist to just under the bust on the bodice, and from the waist to just above the hipline on the skirt. Do not allow the new lines to reach the bust dart or the hipline, because the bust and hip measurements should not be disturbed.

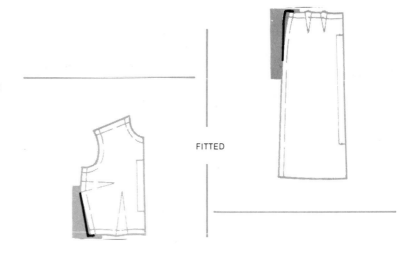

FITTED

Fitted skirts

For a gored skirt, enlarge the waist at the side seams as explained for princess style garments.

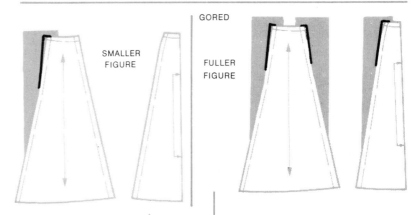

GORED

SMALLER FIGURE

FULLER FIGURE

Unfitted skirts

For a circular skirt, draw a new waist seamline one-fourth of the amount needed below the existing waist edge; follow the curve of the pattern so that the style line is maintained. Then draw a new cutting line. On a semicircular skirt which has no hip shaping, the waist can be increased in a manner similar to that explained for princess style garments.

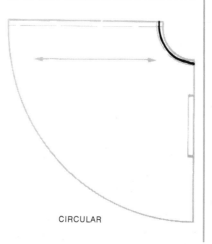

CIRCULAR

Waistband

Enlarge the waistband of a separate skirt the full amount, making half the adjustment at center front and back or at the side seam markings.

WAISTBAND

54

REDUCING THE HIPS

Patterns purchased by bust measurement may not fit smoothly across the hips and must be adjusted if the skirt section is not to be distorted. A smooth hip fit draws attention away from hips that are disproportionately small, thus bringing the figure back into proportion visually.

A garment that hangs loosely over the hip area while fitting perfectly in the bust and waist area is not flattering; the pattern must be adjusted. By comparing your personal measurements to those of the pattern, you will arrive at the amount of hip adjustment you need. Unless the waistline is also reduced, avoid making adjustments of more than 2" (5cm) since it will tend to destroy the design of the garment.

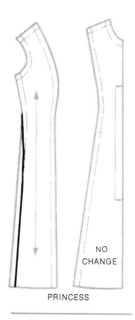

1" (25MM) OR LESS

NO CHANGE

PRINCESS

A-line dresses

1" (25MM) OR LESS

On an A-line style, the hip should not be reduced more than 1" (25mm), as the style lines of your fashion may be distorted. To reduce 1" (25mm) or Less, mark one-fourth of the amount needed to be reduced at the hipline. Draw new seam and cutting lines, tapering from the hipline to just below waist. From the hipline to the hem, keep the adjustment even, taking from the lower edge the same amount subtracted from the hipline.

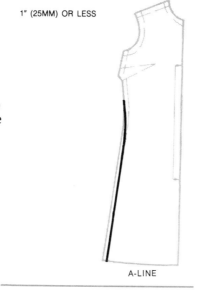

A-LINE

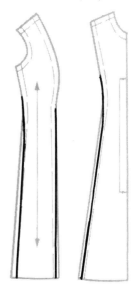

UP TO 2" (5CM)

PRINCESS

Princess dresses

1" (25mm) or Less: Mark one-fourth of the total adjustment necessary at the hipline at the side seam. Draw new cutting lines, tapering from the hipline to just below the waist indication on the pattern. From the hipline to the hem, keep the amount to be reduced equal in width. Reduce the hem circumference the same amount as the hipline was reduced.

Up to 2" (5cm): Divide the amount to be reduced by the number of seams, excluding the center front and center back seams. Halve this figure in order to find the appropriate amount needed to be reduced at each seam edge. Mark this amount at the hipline. Draw new cutting lines, tapering from the hipline to just under the waist. Keep the amount to be reduced equal from the hipline to the lower edge of the pattern.

55

Fitted dresses

For a style with a waist seam, mark one-fourth of the amount needed to be reduced at the hipline indication. Draw new cutting lines, tapering from the hipline to just below the waist. From the hipline to the lower edge keep the amount even.

Fitted skirts

1″ (25mm) or Less: For fitted and gored styles, follow the instructions for fitted dresses, tapering from the hipline to just below the waist.

Up to 2″ (5cm): For gored skirt styles, the adjustment is distributed evenly among all seams. For styles with only two side seams, follow the instructions for fitted dresses, tapering from the hipline to just below the waist.

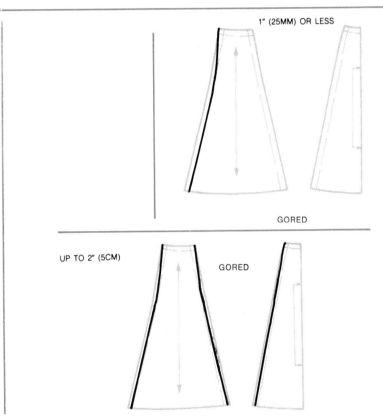

FITTED

1″ (25MM) OR LESS

GORED

UP TO 2″ (5CM)   GORED

Unfitted skirts

Gathered or circular styles with no fitting through the hip area will need no adjustment in the hip area of the pattern.

ENLARGING THE HIPS

Large hips are a common figure problem among women. A skirt that covers your contours and does not pull or ride up can deemphasize large hips. Never use wearing ease to accommodate large hips, as this will distort both style and fit.

A-line dresses

2″ (5cm) or Less: Follow the instructions for fitted dresses.

More than 2″ (5cm): Slash the pattern parallel to the grainline up to and across the hipline, as illustrated. Place tissue paper under the slash, spreading the pattern one-fourth of the amount needed. Pin, check, and tape. Draw new cutting lines, tapering to the bust area.

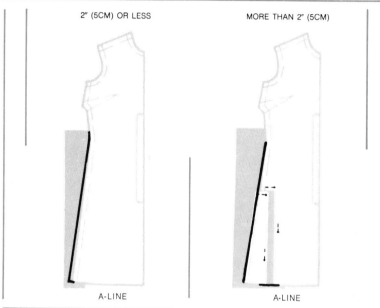

2″ (5CM) OR LESS   MORE THAN 2″ (5CM)

A-LINE   A-LINE

Princess dresses

2″ (5cm) or Less: Follow the instructions for fitted dresses.

More than 2″ (5cm): Divide the amount needed by the number of seams, excluding center front and center back seams. Halve this figure to get the amount needed at each seam edge. Place tissue paper at the edges. Mark the amount needed at the hipline and lower edges. Draw new cutting lines, tapering from the hip to just below the waist indication.

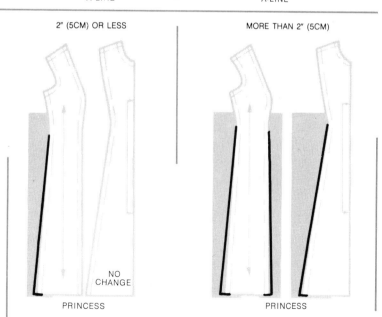

2″ (5CM) OR LESS   MORE THAN 2″ (5CM)

NO CHANGE

PRINCESS   PRINCESS

57

Fitted dresses

2″ (5cm) or Less: For designs with a waist seam, add tissue paper to the side edges. Mark one-fourth of the amount needed to enlarge at the full hipline. Draw new cutting lines, tapering from the waist to the hipline, and keeping the enlargement even from the hipline to the lower edge.

More than 2″ (5cm): For a design with a waist seam, slash the pattern parallel to the grainline, as shown. Place tissue paper under the slash, and spread the pattern one-fourth of the amount needed; pin. Check the adjustment and fasten with tape. Draw in new cutting lines. To remove excess waist circumference, draw an additional dart as shown, or reduce the waist at the side seams as explained on pages 51-52.

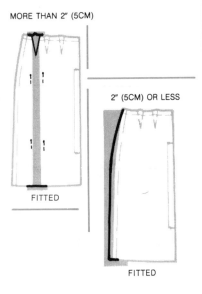

MORE THAN 2″ (5CM)

FITTED

2″ (5CM) OR LESS

FITTED

Fitted skirts

2″ (5cm) or Less: For fitted, gored, and slim gathered styles, follow the instructions for fitted dresses, tapering from the waist to the hipline.

More than 2″ (5cm): For fitted and slim gathered styles, slash as for a fitted dress and add a dart if necessary.

For a gored skirt, divide the amount needed to be enlarged by the number of seams, excluding the center front and center back seams. Halve this amount to find the adjustment needed at each seam edge. Add tissue paper to the side edges. Mark the needed amount at the hipline and hem. Then draw new seam and cutting lines, tapering from the waist to the hipline, and keeping the amount even from the hipline to the lower edge of the pattern.

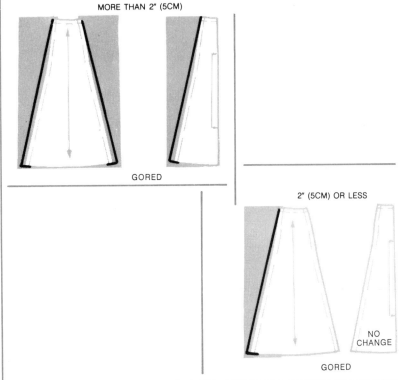

MORE THAN 2″ (5CM)

GORED

2″ (5CM) OR LESS

NO CHANGE

GORED

Unfitted skirts

2″ (5cm) or Less: For a skirt with a natural waist seam that is unfitted through the hip area, like a circular or gathered skirt, no hip adjustment is needed. However, if it has a hip seam, enlarge it as you would a fitted style.

More than 2″ (5cm): Same as above.

SPECIAL SITUATIONS

Combining adjustments

When several adjustments have to be made, the length adjustments are always done first, then the circumference adjustments, and finally any specialized adjustments.

Start with those above the waist and work down. Perhaps you need to enlarge the bustline as well as the waistline, but need no adjustment at the hipline. One adjustment could affect another, so always proceed from top to bottom.

Measure and mark the adjustment needed at each area of the body and draw new cutting lines tapering from the bustline to the waistline to the hipline.

If the pattern needs to be slashed, do one section at a time, then join the pieces and redraw any interrupted lines.

Intricate pattern pieces

A pattern with unusual seaming may make a simple adjustment appear complicated. You may have to analyze the pattern design and make some common sense decisions about making the adjustment. Remember, the most important consideration is to

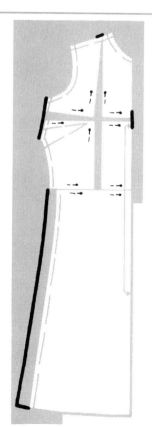
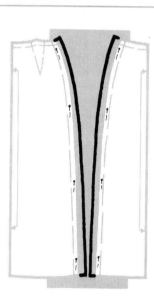

achieve a flattering fit without distorting the design of the pattern. For instance, a skirt pattern with two front seams, two back seams and no side seams should be adjusted evenly along the existing seams.

A skirt pattern with a yolk, diagonal seams, or several horizontal seams will have to be adjusted proportionately on each piece.

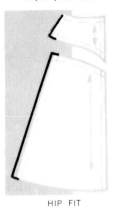

2" (5CM) OR LESS

HIP FIT

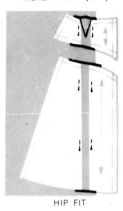

MORE THAN 2" (5CM)

HIP FIT

Uneven adjustments

Most often, your body contour is not identical on the right and left sides. The differences are usually so minor that it requires no special fitting accommodations. However, if you have a figure with substantial differences, you will want to adjust the pattern to fit each side. You may want to make a fitting shell to more accurately fit your body.

Adjust the pattern to fit the larger side, and with a contrasting color pen, mark the stitching line for the smaller side right on the tissue. When you cut your fabric, you can still cut a double thickness to fit the larger side, and then simply trim away the excess or mark the stitching line on the smaller side afterward.

4 *The Basic Fitting Shell*

Now that you know how to make basic length and circumference adjustments, you may have all the facts necessary for a perfect fit. But if you need more than the basic pattern adjustments, or if you want additional knowledge of fitting techniques, you may want to make a fitting shell. A fitting shell is made for the sole purpose of solving fitting problems. After the shell has been adjusted and altered to fit you perfectly, the adjustments you have made can be transferred to any Vogue tissue pattern.

The development of this fitting shell will provide you with a perfect sewing tool, saving you time and trouble whenever you sew. You will use it with each new style you make, to check for potential fitting problems before cutting the pattern in fabric, thus avoiding costly mistakes.

Vogue patterns offer two ways to make a fitting shell:

☐ The Vogue Professional Fitting Program #1001 contains a master pattern which is printed on non-woven fabric. The master pattern has all the necessary markings printed on it to make adjusting and altering your pattern easy. You simply alter the master pattern and then fit it to your body. Complete instructions for adjusting and altering the master pattern are included with the program. When using this program, you do not need to purchase additional fabric.

☐ The Vogue Basic Fitting Shell #1004 is a tissue pattern used to make a fitting shell. You purchase muslin or gingham fabric to complete the shell. If you are using this pattern to make a fitting shell, use the following information to prepare your fabric.

Making the Basic Fitting Shell

The classic fitting shell is a closely fitted dress with a waistline seam. It is often called a muslin, as this is the traditional fabric from which the shell is made. However, you might choose to use a good, firmly woven gingham since the checks can be extremely helpful for keeping grainlines straight. Actually, any firmly woven medium-weight fabric is satisfactory as long as the fabric is grain-perfect. You will also need a zipper.

Shrink the fabric or press it thoroughly with a steam iron.

Adjust the grain. Every woven fabric consists of crosswise and lengthwise threads (which are more sturdy). Grain is the direction in which they run. Preparation of the grain is of vital importance to the look of your finished garment. A garment cut off the grain will twist and sag across the center or at one or both sides.

Straighten the fabric ends by snipping the selvage and pulling a crosswise thread until the fabric puckers. Cut along the puckered line across the entire width.

To straighten the grain, pull the fabric in the opposite direction from the way the ends slant, until a perfect right-angle corner is formed.

The fabric is on grain when lengthwise and crosswise threads are at a perfect right angle to each other.

When the grainline is straight, mark it with a pencil on the wrong side of the fabric. Mark the lengthwise grain along the center, and the crosswise grain every half yard. It will not be necessary to mark grainlines if you use a woven gingham fabric for your muslin.

Adjust your "Vogue Basic Fitting Shell" to your measurements; be sure to use the straight skirt rather than the A-line skirt which is also included in the pattern. Arrange the fabric as indicated by your cutting layout; pin the selvages together, matching your crosswise grain markings. The fabric must be on grain before you pin the pattern pieces to it. Cut out your muslin shell carefully; even the addition of ⅛" (3mm) can distort the fit.

Using a tracing wheel and dressmaker's tracing paper, transfer all construction and position lines from your fitting pattern to your muslin. Mark seamlines, darts, bustline, and hipline. Seamlines and darts should be marked on the wrong side of the fabric; you can mark the bustline, hipline, and crosswise grain of sleeves on the right side with tracing wheel and paper, or you can mark them on the wrong side and transfer them to the right side with thread tracing after the pattern pieces have been removed. Make sure your thread tracing is clearly visible; choose one color for position lines and other colors for the lengthwise grain, center folds, and crosswise grain.

Follow the pattern sewing instructions when making your muslin fitting garment. Stitch the garment sections together with machine basting so changes can be made with relative ease. Stitch the neck and lower edges of sleeves along the seamlines. Turn in the edges along the stitching; clip as necessary, then baste and press. The zipper is machine basted in place so you will be able to try on and fit your muslin shell easily.

Shaping the Basic Fitting Shell

Your basic fitting shell can be the key to solving your fitting problems if you understand the procedure for altering the shell to perfection. The shell is a fitting tool, so don't hesitate to mark it, cut it, or experiment with it. Use this section as an encyclopedia and refer to those alterations required by your figure. Shape and mold the basic fitting shell to the contours of your body as you work to achieve a flattering fit.

  If you have chosen not to make a fitting shell, these alterations will also provide a guide for perfecting the fit of your fashion garment. The procedures for altering specific designs such as those with yokes, extended shoulders, and raglan or kimono sleeves have been included here for your convenience. Naturally it will not be possible to slash into the fabric as you can with your fitting shell; but if the alteration is minor, you'll be able to correct it in the seams. Refer to Chapter 5 for information on fitting your fashion garment.

SHOULDERS

Begin with the shoulders in shaping your fitting shell to the contours of your body and in keeping the direction of the grainlines correct. When the grain is correct in the shoulder area, it is a good indication that your fitting shell will hang straight from the shoulders. There may be other body areas that distort the direction of the grain, but these flaws are more easily remedied if the proper grain has been established in the shoulder area. The shoulder seams should be directly on top of the shoulders and end at the base of the neck.

Square

Caused by bone structure, this variation is evidenced by pulling around the shoulder and armhole area because the garment is not wide enough to accommodate your body. Remove the sleeve and slash both front and back bodice sections near the shoulder seam from armhole edge to neck seamline. By adding the necessary amount of fabric equally—half the amount needed in the back, and half in the front—you retain the proper positioning of the shoulder seam and the original direction of the grain. Spread the cut edges the amount needed for proper fit; smooth any wrinkles as you mold the fabric. Insert strips of fabric under the cut edges and baste. Trim the strips even with the armhole edge. Raise the armhole the amount added to the shoulder area and reshape. Correct the length and position of any back shoulder darts so that they originate in the center of the shoulder and point to the shoulder blade. Transfer the alterations to the pattern.

To alter a yoke, slash along the shoulder marking to the neck seamline. Alter raglan sleeves and princess styles as illustrated. For a kimono sleeve, slash across the pattern so you can raise the shoulder curves; correct the armhole curve.

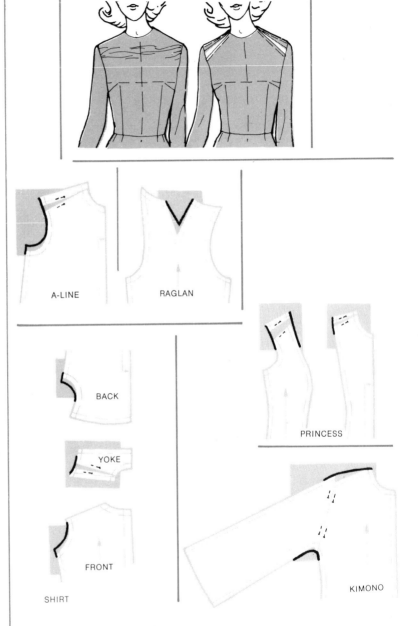

A-LINE

RAGLAN

BACK

YOKE

FRONT

SHIRT

PRINCESS

KIMONO

Sloping

Sloping shoulders may be more apparent when combined with poor posture, but they are essentially caused by the angle of the shoulder bone in relation to the neck and the arm. The fabric wrinkles near the bust dart and across the end of the shoulder in the back. These wrinkles are easily eliminated by molding the fabric to the correct angle of your shoulder and shaping the armhole to the set of your arm.

There are two methods of correcting this problem. First, try shoulder pads of varying shapes, widths, and thicknesses. You may find that is enough to correct the fit. If the problem is severe, you can combine shoulder pads with a slight shoulder alteration. You will find this more flattering than trying to correct by alteration alone, which only accentuates the problem.

For set-in sleeves, remove the sleeve. Pin out the excess at the shoulder, tapering to the neck seamline. Lower the armhole seamline the same amount as the excess fabric removed from the shoulder. This reshaping retains the original size of the armhole and does not change the fit of the set-in sleeve. Correct the length and position of any back shoulder darts so that they originate in the center of the shoulder and point to the shoulder blade. Transfer the alterations to your pattern.

To alter a garment design with a yoke, slash along the

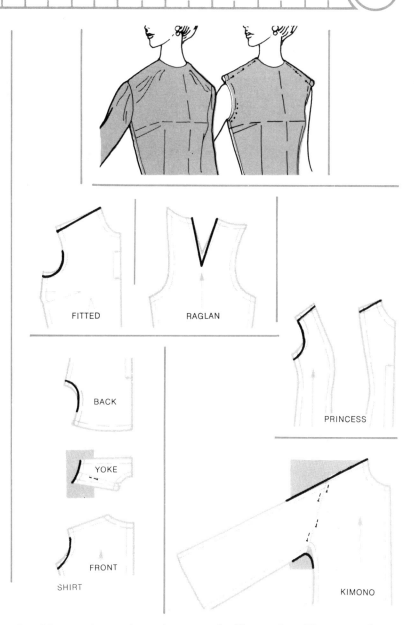

FITTED

RAGLAN

BACK

YOKE

FRONT

SHIRT

PRINCESS

KIMONO

shoulder markings from the armhole edge to the neck seamline to reduce the amount needed. Reshape the armhole as you did for a set-in sleeve. For raglan sleeves and princess-style garments, alter the pattern piece as indicated in the illustration. However, for the kimono sleeve, first slash across pattern so you can reduce the shoulder curve more easily, and then correct the armhole curve to fit properly.

Narrow

This alteration is necessitated by bone structure too, and the fitting shell must be taken in at the front shoulder area as well as the back. In set-in sleeves, the armhole seams fall beyond the shoulder point; other sleeve styles wrinkle across the upper arm and sometimes restrict movement. Correct set-in sleeve designs by pinning a dart in the front and back, pulling the armhole seam to the correct position. Alter the pattern pieces the same amount.

To alter a yoke with a set-in sleeve, slash midway through the yoke along the shoulder markings and through the yoke and into the front and back sections diagonally from the shoulder line; you must decrease the shoulder length. Make a fold, tapering to nothing at the armhole seamline. Alter other sleeve types and style variations as shown.

Sometimes an alteration of this type will make your proportions appear triangular. A soft shoulder pad placed in the garment so that the edge extends slightly beyond the shoulder seam and into the sleeve may be a more flattering solution than altering the garment. Also, choosing styles with a slight fullness or puff in the sleeve area may flatter the figure with narrow shoulders.

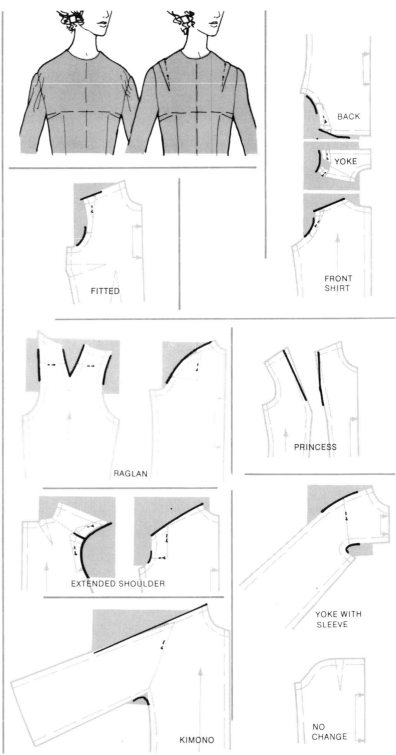

BACK

YOKE

FRONT SHIRT

FITTED

RAGLAN

PRINCESS

EXTENDED SHOULDER

YOKE WITH SLEEVE

KIMONO

NO CHANGE

Broad

The alteration is needed to accommodate bone structure. Set-in sleeve styles are pulled at the sleeve cap as the armhole seams are drawn up over broad shoulders. Other sleeve styles are pulled in the armhole area and movement is restricted. Correct your fitting shell by slashing front and back sections from a point midway along the shoulder to the armhole seam. Spread the cut edges until the shoulder area is smooth and properly molded. Insert fabric strips under the cut edges and baste.

For a yoke alteration with set-in sleeves, slash midway through the yoke at the shoulder markings and again from the shoulder to the armhole seamline of front and back sections. Spread as needed. Alter pattern pieces as illustrated for other sleeve types and style variations.

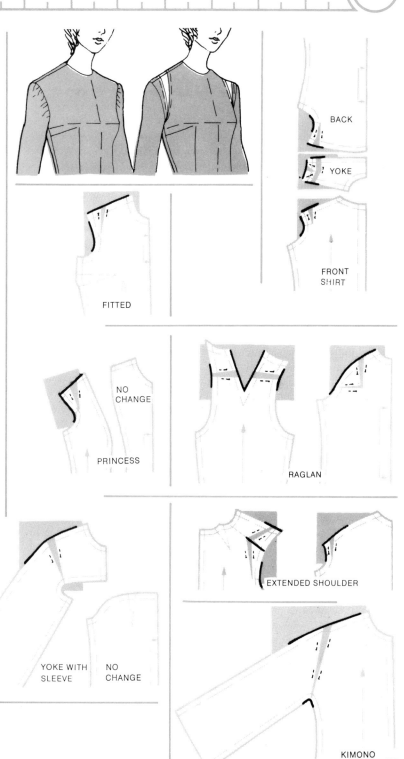

FITTED

BACK

YOKE

FRONT
SHIRT

PRINCESS

NO
CHANGE

RAGLAN

YOKE WITH
SLEEVE

NO
CHANGE

EXTENDED SHOULDER

KIMONO

NECKLINES

A neckline is often a primary focal point of your garment. What the rest of your garment does for your body, the neckline does for your face. To flatter you, it must not only be an appropriate style but also a superb fit. A neckline that constricts or hangs away from you is not attractive or flattering to your face or to the garment.

The base of your neck is the point from which any garment neckline is designed. A variety of conditions—large or small bust cup size, hollow chest, broad shoulders, etc.—can cause the neckline to fit poorly. The effects can be corrected with the following alterations.

Tight

The neckline pulls and cuts into the neck. The top edge of your garment reaches far above the base of the neck, binding and stretching your fabric. To bring the neckline into position, draw a line on the fabric where the neckline of the fitting shell should be, and stitch along this line. Clip to this line every ½" (13mm) until it is comfortable. Transfer your alteration to your pattern (alter facings as well) by drawing in new cutting lines the distance of the new seamline from the original. Make the same alterations in set-in-sleeve garments with yokes, and in raglan- and kimono-sleeve garments that have jewel necklines.

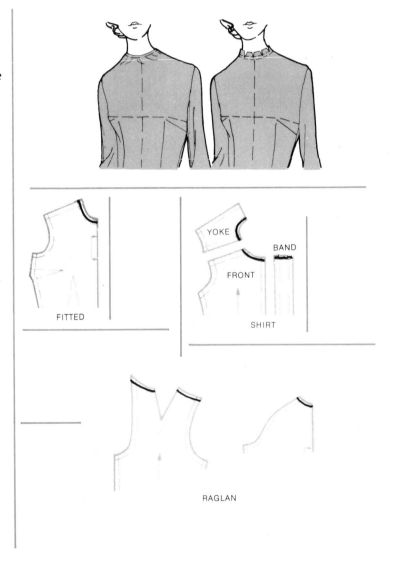

YOKE

BAND

FRONT

FITTED

SHIRT

RAGLAN

Gaping

Carefully check the bodice to locate the problem—both gaping and pulling can be present concurrently. Even though your pattern is purchased by bust measurement, your bust cup size or body contours may still distort the neckline. Often a combination of alterations is necessary to fit the neckline properly; the problem here would be also evident in square, V- or U-necklines.

Too much fabric causes the neckline to stand away from the body in wrinkles above the bust. Smooth out the wrinkles and pin, tapering to the armhole seam. To make the changes on your pattern, lower the cutting line at the shoulder half the amount needed, tapering to the armhole seam. Raise the center front the other half of the amount needed. Make the same change on the facing. Alter similarly for garments with raglan and kimono sleeves.

Sometimes the armhole seam will pull and distorts the neckline above the bust. To alter, release the armhole seam in that area and slash the fabric from where it pulls at the arm-

hole to the neck seamline. Spread the fabric as needed, and baste in strips of fabric. Rebaste the sleeve to test. Alter your pattern by slashing in the same manner. Make the same change on the facing. Alter garments with raglan and kimono sleeves similarly.

Too little fabric to cover the bust contour will cause the neckline to pull and gape. The bodice front must be altered to bring the neckline into correct position. Refer to the alteration for the large bust cup on page 84. Maintain your bodice design in correcting the fit.

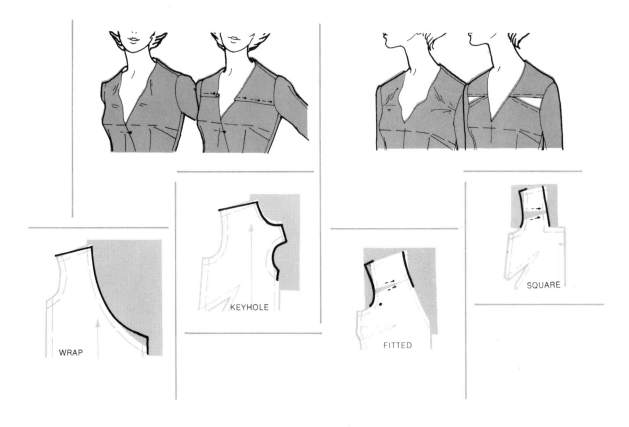

WRAP

KEYHOLE

FITTED

SQUARE

Large

The neckline hangs loosely and does not reach the base of the neck. To raise the neckline, baste a folded shaped bias strip of fabric in the correct position. Alter the bodice front as indicated, making the same change on the bodice back and facings. You can apply the same alteration to a yoke garment with a set-in sleeve, and to raglan- and kimono-sleeve garments with a jewel neckline.

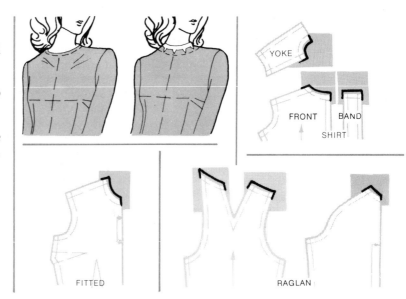

YOKE

FRONT   BAND

SHIRT

FITTED

RAGLAN

Décolleté

To test the position of the neckline before you cut into your fashion fabric, make a muslin neck facing. Stitch along the seamline, turn in the neck edges along the stitching, and clip every ½″ (13mm); baste. Try on the facing, checking to see how deep the neckline is. To raise the neckline, fill it in with a piece of fabric until the desired depth is achieved. Redraw cutting lines on the facing and bodice front, maintaining the style lines.

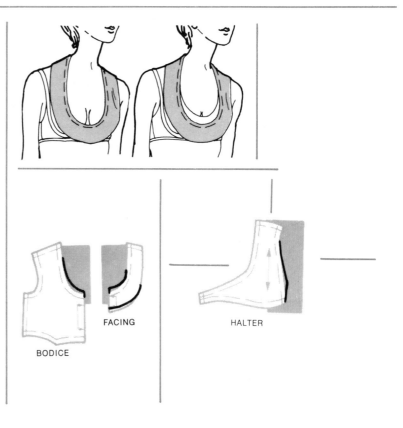

FACING

HALTER

BODICE

70

ARMHOLES

Although your basic fitting shell has a set-in sleeve, there are many sleeveless styles— close-fitting armholes, cut-away armholes, and halter variations. Alterations required in the armhole area may be the result of poor fit in other areas. Proper fit in the shoulder area, as well as in the back, chest, and bust areas, should be achieved before altering the armhole area.

Cut-away armholes and the armhole area of a halter neckline are not as close to the arm, and the shape is not the same as a close-fitting sleeveless armhole. There is little or no wearing ease in the shoulder and side underarm seams, as the fit of these armholes depends largely upon the support of the body.

Test the fit of an armhole by stitching along the armhole seamline. Turn the seam allowance to the inside along the stitching and clip at ½" to ¾" (15mm to 20mm) intervals; baste. Try on the bodice and check the underarm portion— the classic sleeveless armhole should fit close to the body and should be 1" (25mm) below the armpit. The rest of the armhole should fit smoothly without pulling, binding, or restricting movement.

Tight

If the armhole is too tight it will bind and pull from the underarm to below the shoulder. Redraw the armhole seamline farther into the body of the garment on front and back sections where the binding occurs. Remove bodice and basting stitches. Stitch carefully along the new seamline and clip at ½" (13mm) intervals; baste. Try on the bodice once more to see that no further alterations are necessary, and that the new armhole is smooth and comfortable. Transfer the alteration to the bodice and facing pattern pieces as illustrated.

Alter the pattern of a cut-away armhole and the armhole area of a halter as indicated in the illustration.

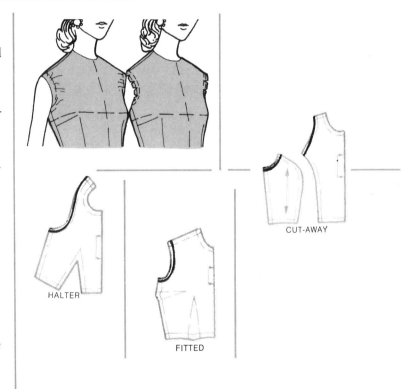

HALTER

FITTED

CUT-AWAY

Large

In sleeveless styles this alteration is required primarily in the
underarm area when the armhole is too deep. In styles with
sleeves, movement is re-
stricted, and the garment feels
tight. To correct, insert bias
strips of fabric to fill in the
amount needed around and
under the arm. When these
strips are placed accurately,
they should produce an even
extension of the underarm
seam, as well as retain the
proper curve of the armhole.
Baste the strips securely in
place. Transfer the alteration to
the bodice and sleeve or facing
pattern pieces.
   Alter the pattern of a cut-
away armhole and the armhole
area of a halter as indicated in
the illustration.

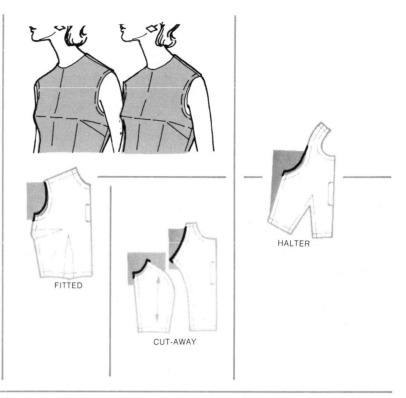

FITTED

CUT-AWAY

HALTER

Gaping

Even though your fitting shell
bodice fits smoothly in the
shoulders, further alteration of
this area may be required if the
armhole gapes. For a closer
armhole fit, pin out excess fabric at the shoulder to bring the
armhole into place. Taper the
shoulder seam to the neck. If
this alteration does not correct
the armhole, you may have to
further raise the underarm by
inserting bias strips, as you
would in altering a large armhole.
   Alter the pattern of a cut-
away armhole and the armhole
area of a halter as indicated in
the illustration.

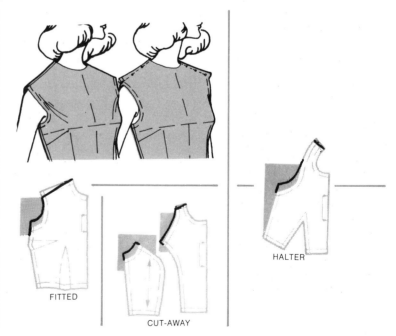

FITTED

CUT-AWAY

HALTER

SLEEVES

Since sleeves are an integral part of your garment, they should fit well and be visually pleasing. Countless variations of sleeves can be found in the Vogue Patterns catalogues. Sleeves are grouped into three types: set-in, joined with a seam that encircles the arm near the shoulder; raglan, with diagonal seaming that extends to the neck edge; and kimono, cut-in-one with the garment.

Set-in sleeve versions are innumerable: the classic one- or two-piece sleeve in any length you may choose, as well as the shirt, bishop, angel, bell, and trumpet styles which usually have a smooth sleeve cap. These can also be gathered in the sleeve cap area and anywhere along the arm to create a puff sleeve or can be combined with a fitted sleeve to create a leg-of-mutton sleeve.

Raglan sleeves can be one- or two-piece, and are great problem solvers for hard-to-fit shoulders. Not only can a good fit be achieved with these sleeves, but they involve less handling during construction than the other types.

Kimono sleeves exist in nearly as many variations as the set-in: they can be used with gussets for a high-fitting armhole, or can be cut without a shoulder and upper arm seam for loose, flowing styles. There is the cap sleeve version, a yoke cut-in-one with any length of sleeve, the dolman, the bat-wing, etc.

With a better understanding of sleeves, you will certainly approach them with greater awareness. Once you have worked out your problems in the three basic types it will be a simple matter to alter any of the variations. It should not surprise you that there are as many different types of arms as there are deviations from standard body measurements.

Often body fit on a pattern is refined to satisfaction, yet the sleeves are neglected because fitting them is considered difficult and troublesome. This is unfortunate, as sleeve fit is an integral part of perfect fit and is not complicated at all. Frequently, sleeve fit is distorted by nothing more than the ease distribution of the sleeve cap being inappropriate for your body contour or bone structure. The sleeves of Vogue patterns are designed for a standard figure; you must individualize your pattern by building in your own sleeve fit.

Ease distribution

Simple to correct, this problem is visible when the upper sleeve area will not lie smoothly, and diagonal wrinkles form at the front or back of the sleeve cap and continue across the sleeve, distorting the lengthwise grain. To alter, release the sleeve between the notches. For wrinkles that start at the front of the sleeve cap, adjust the ease, shifting it toward the front until the wrinkles are

eliminated. For wrinkles that start at the back, redistributing it until the wrinkles have been eliminated. To check the alteration you have made, baste the sleeve into the armhole and examine it with care. The upper sleeve area should now be smooth.

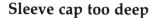

Skimpy sleeve cap

The sleeve cap is too short, causing it to pull and collapse, creating wrinkles. Remove the sleeve between the notches, and slash across the sleeve. Place a piece of fabric under the cut edges, spreading the amount needed to increase the cap. Rebaste to check. Alter the pattern as indicated.

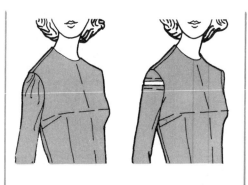

FITTED

Sleeve cap too deep

Wrinkles appear across the top of the sleeve cap just under the seam. To correct, pin out the excess fabric until it lies flat. On the pattern, fold out the same amount on the sleeve cap. You should expect to have less ease in the cap as a result of this correction.

FITTED

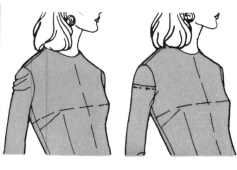

Excess ease

Wrinkles appear in the sleeve cap around the armhole seam, distorting the sleeve shape. Release the stitching between the notches at the sleeve cap. Smooth out the wrinkles and pin in a shallow vertical dart. Baste the sleeve in place. To correct the pattern, make a 3" to 4" (7.5cm to 10cm) slash at the shoulder marking, and lap the edges the amount to be decreased. The pattern will bulge slightly; to make the seam allowances lie flat, clip 1½" (3.8cm) at each end of the eased area. Check to make sure the circumference of the sleeve is preserved under the eased area. Shorten the sleeve cap slightly by drawing a new cutting line.

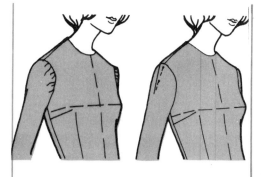

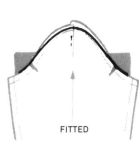

FITTED

Large arm

A fitted sleeve that is not altered to fit a large arm will
have absolutely no wearing
ease and will be uncomfortable. The sleeve will pull and
bind due to lack of sufficient
fabric. Even though the armhole is adequate, there still is
not enough room for a well-de-
veloped or fleshy arm. To
enlarge the sleeve, slash along
the lengthwise grain. Spread
the slash over a strip of fabric
as needed, allowing for wearing ease and tapering to the
shoulder seam and to the
sleeve edge. If, when enlarging
the circumference, the sleeve
cap is still distorted, alter the
sleeve cap as you would for a
skimpy sleeve cap, page 74.
Test the alterations. When altering the pattern, form tucks
as shown to make the pattern
lie flat. Redraw the sleeve cap
and grainlines.

Stylized versions of the set-in
sleeve such as the bell or shirt
will need this alteration too.
Alter a raglan sleeve in the
same way. A gathered shirt
sleeve with a cuff can be altered in both girth and length
to create a longer, fuller sleeve
that is more in proportion with
your figure. To enlarge a
kimono sleeve, add half the
amount needed to both front
and back seam edges as illustrated.

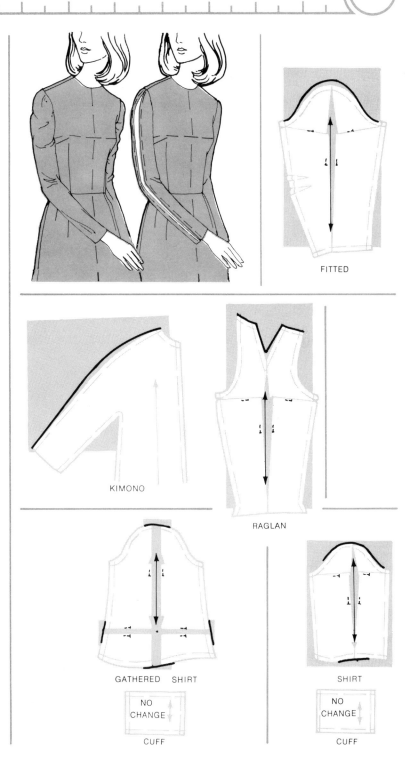

FITTED

KIMONO

RAGLAN

GATHERED SHIRT

CUFF / NO CHANGE

SHIRT

CUFF / NO CHANGE

Thin arm

A fitted sleeve on a thin arm
will wrinkle and sag. Wearing
ease becomes bagginess and
the sleeve has no shape. While
the too-large sleeve may feel
comfortable, its appearance will
ruin your fashion impact. To
correct, make a lengthwise fold
along the lengthwise grain,
starting at the sleeve cap and
tapering to the lower edge. Be
sure there is enough width to
allow the hand to slip through
the sleeves if no opening is
provided. To transfer the alteration to the pattern, make
an identical change. Sleeve
ease will be somewhat lessened
by the fold.

Style variations of the set-in
sleeve, such as the shirt or
bishop, will need this alteration
too. A gathered shirt sleeve can
be altered in both girth and
length to create a narrower and
shorter sleeve that is more in
proportion with your figure. To
reduce a raglan sleeve, make a
fold from the dart to the sleeve
edge. On a kimono sleeve, reduce both seam edges as
shown, halving the amount
needed and making an equal
adjustment on both the front
and back.

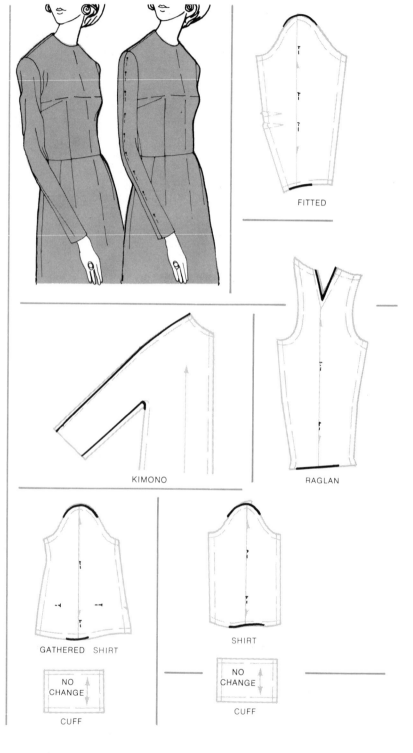

FITTED

KIMONO

RAGLAN

GATHERED SHIRT

SHIRT

NO CHANGE

CUFF

NO CHANGE

CUFF

Large upper arm

A sleeve inadequate for a large upper arm will be snug above the elbow and the armhole seam will bind. Wearing ease will be nonexistent, and the look will be distorted. To correct, release the stitching between the notches on the sleeve cap. Slash along the grainline and insert a strip of fabric under the slash. Spread the sleeve the amount needed—allow wearing ease as well—and baste. Extend the ease on the sleeve cap 1″ to 2″ (2.5cm to 5cm) beyond the markings so it will be well distributed; rebaste the sleeve into the armhole. Try on the fitting shell to check the fit. If you find the armhole seam still binds, refer to page 64 and make the alteration for square shoulders. Transfer the alteration to the fitting pattern, redrawing the grainline as indicated.

Make the same alteration for a short sleeve or a slim shirt sleeve with a cuff, and a raglan sleeve. To alter a kimono sleeve, slash at the shoulder indication and down as shown, adding half the amount needed to the front and half to the back.

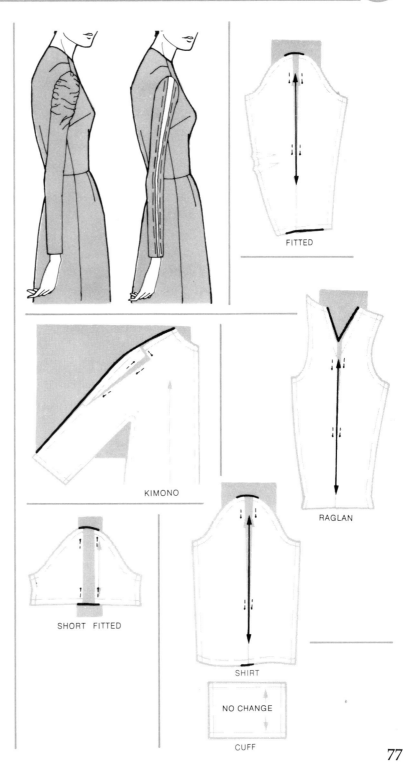

FITTED

KIMONO

SHORT FITTED

SHIRT

NO CHANGE

CUFF

RAGLAN

Thick elbow

Although ease, shape, or darts
in fitted sleeves allow elbow
movement, often the sleeve
just cannot accommodate a
large, thick elbow. The sleeve
pulls from the shoulder and is
uncomfortable. At the elbow itself, the fit is tight and binding.
To correct, release the stitching
between the notches on the
sleeve seam. Starting between
the darts, slash to the
grainline, then continue upward along the grainline to the
sleeve cap edge. Place strips of
fabric under the slashed edges
and spread the amount
needed; baste. To take up extra
fabric at the sleeve seam, add a
dart between any existing
ones. Restitch the sleeve seam
and try on to check fit. Transfer
the alteration to the pattern,
and draw in the added dart.

To alter stylized set-in sleeves
such as a slim shirt sleeve with
a cuff, slash as indicated in the
illustration. Alter a raglan or
kimono sleeve pattern in the
same manner, slashing through
the center of the elbow ease if
darts are not used.

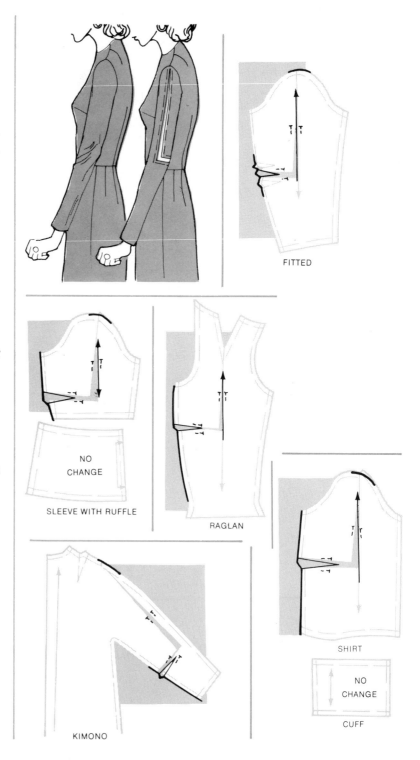

FITTED

NO
CHANGE

SLEEVE WITH RUFFLE

RAGLAN

SHIRT

NO
CHANGE

CUFF

KIMONO

Large forearm

A large forearm will cause the sleeve to pull and bind below the elbow; movement will be restricted on a garment with a fitted sleeve. The fullness of the arm will also use up wearing ease and will emphasize the large forearm. To alter your muslin, slash along the grainline from the lower edge up toward the sleeve cap. Place a fabric strip under the slash and spread the amount needed, adding some wearing ease for ensured comfort. Baste the strip in place and try on to check fit. Transfer the alteration to the pattern.

  For a shorter close-fitting sleeve with fashion detail at the edge, the trim must be adjusted too. For a raglan sleeve, slash along the grainline from the lower edge up to the dart. For a kimono sleeve, add one-fourth the amount needed at each sleeve edge.

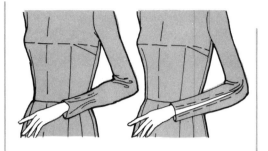

FITTED

KIMONO

RAGLAN

SLEEVE WITH RUFFLE

Small forearm

If a sleeve without stylized trim—like a cuff or band that hugs the wrist—is too large due to a small forearm, it hangs loosely and drapes in wrinkles below the elbow. The sleeve design is distorted and can ruin the lines of the entire garment. To take in the lower sleeve, fold out the excess, tapering the fold up from the lower edge. Always be sure that you have allowed enough room in the sleeve for your hand to slip through. Do not fold out wearing ease. Transfer the alteration to the pattern as illustrated.

Alter a raglan sleeve the same as you would the fitted sleeve.

For a kimono sleeve, mark one-fourth the amount to be decreased at both seam edges; draw in new cutting lines, tapering to the armhole.

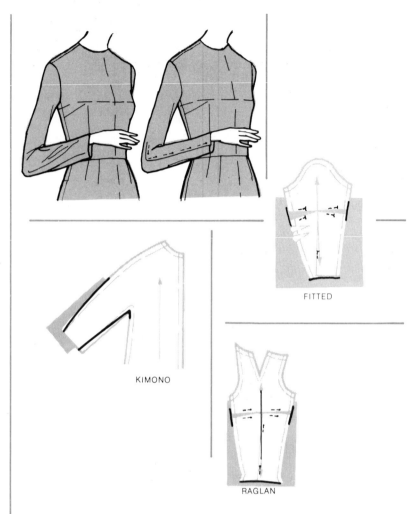

FITTED

KIMONO

RAGLAN

BUST

The bust is one of the most important body areas to be fitted correctly. For this reason, you should buy all your patterns—dresses, blouses, jackets, coats, etc.—by bust measurement to provide the correct circumference for this crucial body area. Other pattern adjustments and alterations can then be made with relative ease.

Even though adequate circumference has been supplied, the bust area may need alterations for other reasons. The position of the bust may be either high or low; your bust cup may be larger or smaller than that of the standard figure; or your proportions may have demanded concessions in pattern size. Before you examine the bust area, check the fit of your shoulders, neckline, sleeves, and armholes. This is the best way to proceed toward your goal of perfect fit, as it takes into consideration the combination of your basic frame and your actual proportions, and the effect that both of these will have on clothing.

Fitting techniques that are based on any other area than the bust make the process more difficult than it has to be. In accommodating the bust with the least amount of fitting, style lines will never be distorted as they would if you bought your patterns to fit your frame, and then attempted to fit this pattern to your actual curves.

Wear proper undergarments when you try on your fitting shell. Evaluate the fit to determine if you need a bustline alteration. Often the contours and bone structure of your back can effect the fit of the bust, making it tight and uncomfortable. If this is the problem, alter the back before proceeding with any bust alterations.

Check the position of the darts. The underarm dart should end ½" (13mm) from the apex and the front darts ½" to 1" (13mm to 25mm) below the apex.

Small cup

Although a pattern may be purchased by bust size, a bust area with a small cup may need to be altered to fit smoothly. Excess fabric causes wrinkles over the bust apex, giving an unkempt appearance. To reduce the bust area on your fitting shell, pin out the excess fabric, making folds parallel and at right angles to the grainline. Be sure to retain wearing ease in both the front and the back. Taper horizontal folds to the side seams and vertical folds to the waist; taper lower for A-line garments. Transfer the alterations to the pattern. On A-line styles, slash through the center of the dart to allow the edges to overlap. If the tapering extends below the waist, add to the seams the amount taken out in the skirt section to preserve hip circumference.

In all darted styles, the darts will become shorter and narrower; fit them to your bust proportions, redrawing as needed.

For styles whose bust shaping is created by seaming details rather than darts, place your altered fitting pattern underneath the pattern as a guide. Reduce the bust by making horizontal and vertical folds, as shown; draw in all broken cutting lines.

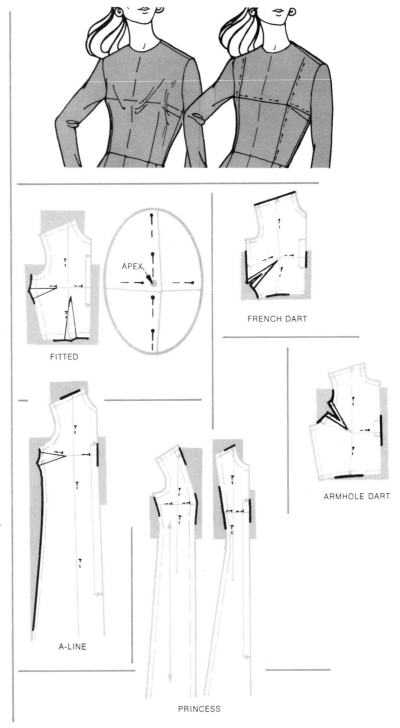

APEX

FITTED

FRENCH DART

ARMHOLE DART

A-LINE

PRINCESS

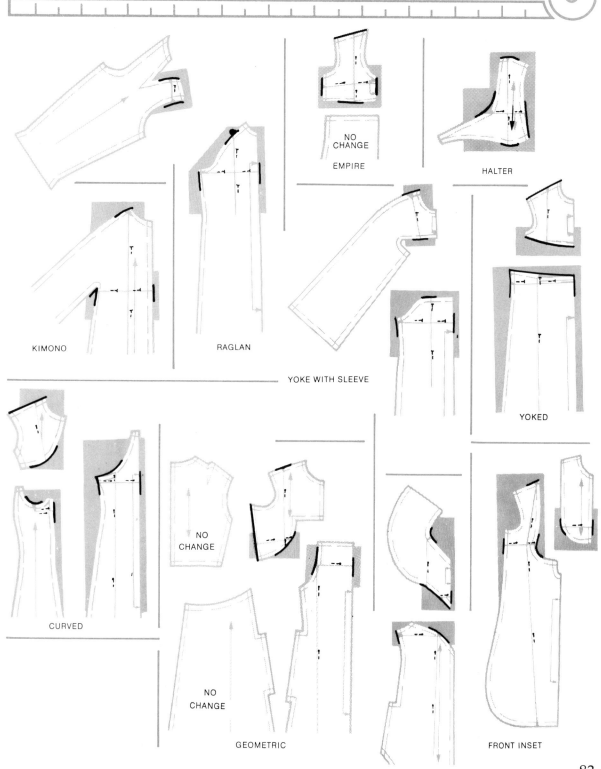

NO
CHANGE

EMPIRE

HALTER

KIMONO

RAGLAN

YOKE WITH SLEEVE

YOKED

NO
CHANGE

CURVED

NO
CHANGE

GEOMETRIC

ONE-PIECE YOKE

FRONT INSET

Large cup

Many women with a large bust cup find that it is necessary to enlarge the bust area of their garments to accommodate the extra fullness. The bodice pulls and is tight across the bust, flattening the apex. To alter your fitting shell to fit your contours, slash through the bust darts and across the front, as shown, at a right angle to the grainline. Slash parallel to the grainline down the front from the shoulder through the apex to the waist seam. Spread the bodice fabric the amount that is needed. Be careful not to overfit. Insert and baste strips of fabric in place. Make the alteration on the pattern in the same manner. Redraw darts, deepening them and changing their length to correspond to your figure. After they are stitched, trim the darts 5/8″ (15mm) from the lines of stitching to reduce the bulk, if necessary. Press the darts open.

To make this alteration in garments whose bust shaping is created by seaming details rather than darts, place your adjusted fitting pattern under your fashion pattern to serve as a guide, adding darts where necessary.

For some garment styles—like princess seaming—divide the amount of change needed between the front and the side fronts. Follow the illustrations in making your alterations.

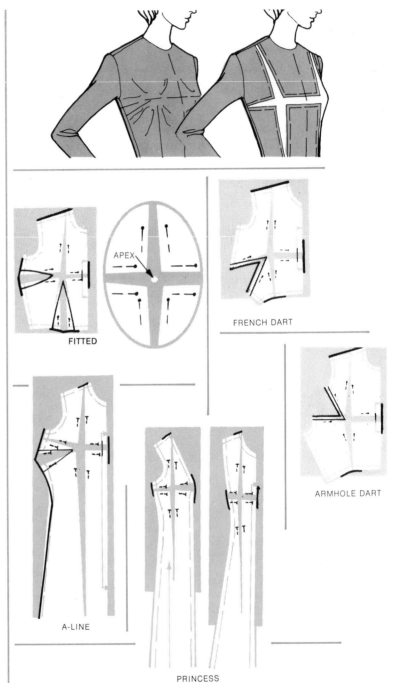

FITTED

APEX

FRENCH DART

ARMHOLE DART

A-LINE

PRINCESS

84

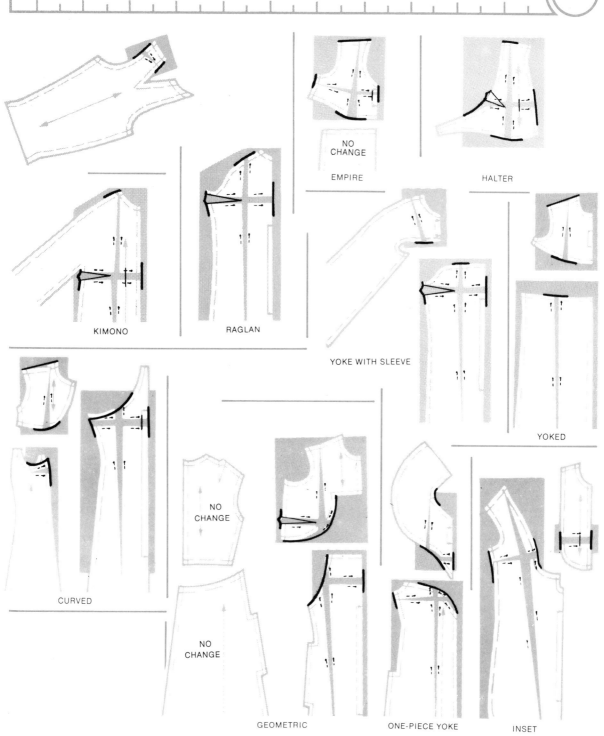

NO
CHANGE

EMPIRE

HALTER

KIMONO

RAGLAN

YOKE WITH SLEEVE

YOKED

CURVED

NO
CHANGE

NO
CHANGE

GEOMETRIC

ONE-PIECE YOKE

INSET

High bust

Your bustline may be too high, in which case you must change the bustline on your fitting shell and pattern. The bust darts will fall too far beneath the bust, and the garment bust shaping will be located beneath your own.

Draw a line across the fitting shell where the bust point should be placed. Open the side seam, release the dart, and restitch it in the new position along your marking; end the darts according to the location of the apex of your bust (see Dart Length, page 88). Raise the front darts as shown. Restitch the side seam and try on the shell to check the correction. This alteration should be applied to all styles with underarm darts, no matter what their angle.

To alter styles that have bust shaping without darts, such as the princess style, place your adjusted fitting pattern under the dartless bodice pieces; this will indicate the bust position. Make a fold, half the amount needed to be raised, above the armhole notch. Slash the pattern below the bust shaping and spread the pattern the same amount. Redraw the shoulder, front, and armhole cutting lines to bring the bodice back to its original shape.
To alter the bustline of other special designs, see the illustrations at right.

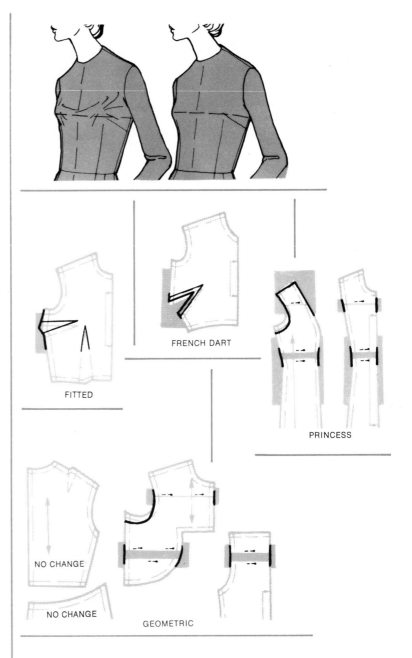

FRENCH DART

FITTED

PRINCESS

NO CHANGE

NO CHANGE

GEOMETRIC

Low bust

You may find that your bust-line is too low for the bust cupping of the fitting shell, and the fit is distorted. Draw a line across your shell where the bust point should be. Release the side seams and the darts. Stitch darts in the proper position, following the marked line and ending the darts in relation to the apex of your bust. Lower the front darts in the same manner. Restitch the side seams, and try on the shell to check the corrected fit. This alteration should be applied to all underarm bust darts, regardless of their angle or the garment style. Correct the dart position on the bodice front.

To alter styles that have bust shaping but no darts—like a princess style—place your altered fitting pattern under the dartless pattern pieces to serve as a guide. Slash through the pattern at the armhole notch and spread the amount needed to lower the bustline. Below the bustline, make a fold half the amount the bustline was lowered, to preserve the bodice length. Raise the armhole below the armhole notch and redraw all other interrupted cutting lines as indicated. To alter the bustline of other designs with special seaming, see the illustration.

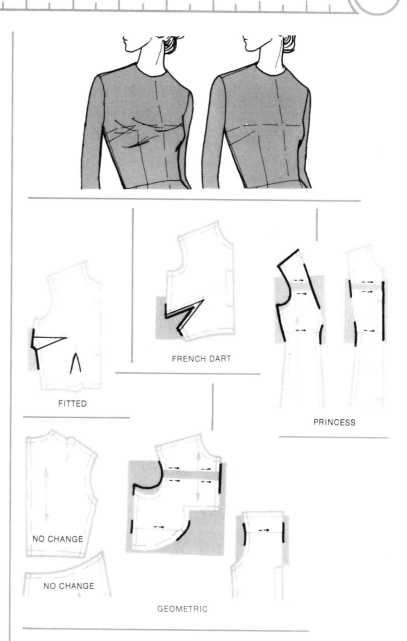

FRENCH DART

FITTED

PRINCESS

NO CHANGE

NO CHANGE

GEOMETRIC

Dart length

If the bust darts on your fitting shell do not fit your contours, you can alter your bodice by re-shaping the darts. The position of the bust apex varies with each woman. The underarm darts should end ½" (13mm) from the apex, and the front darts ½" to 1" (13mm to 25mm) below the apex. Lengthening or shortening darts may not be enough to give a proper fit. Refer to the preceding alterations for high and low bustlines for further instruction.

Styles with bust darts at the armhole can be lengthened or shortened as indicated below.

For French darts, do not cut out the "V" shape when testing. Fit them and then after stitching, trim to within ⅝" (15mm) of the dart seam and press open.

To shorten the underarm dart, place a pin on the fitting shell where the dart should end. Release the side seam and the dart; stitch the dart to the correct length. Restitch the side seam and try on to check the shell. Reposition the bodice front darts the same way.

Transfer the changes to the pattern.

To lengthen the underarm dart, place a pin on the fitting shell where the dart should end. Release the side seam and dart, and shape the underarm dart to your bust contour. Stitch the dart to the correct length. Restitch the side seam and try on the shell to check the correction that you have made. For the bodice front dart, correct the position in the same way. Transfer the changes to your pattern piece as indicated.

TO SHORTEN

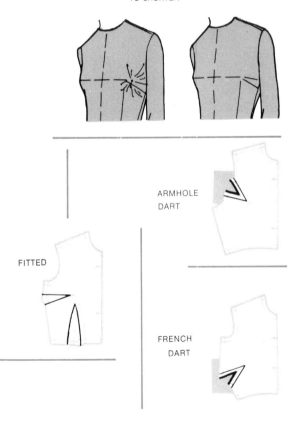

TO LENGTHEN

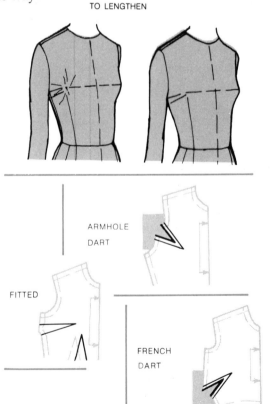

CHEST

Your bone structure is the major cause of alterations in the chest—the rib cage and the collar bone control the length of the bodice. Poor posture or figure flaws may necessitate alterations in the armhole area or between shoulder and bust. These chest alterations affect the front of your garment and should be transferred to related pattern pieces only. Back pattern pieces will not be affected.

Hollow

The bodice wrinkles and gaps between bust and neckline due to excess fabric. To correct, pin out the wrinkles, tapering to armhole or shoulder seams. Transfer the alteration to the bodice front pattern piece.

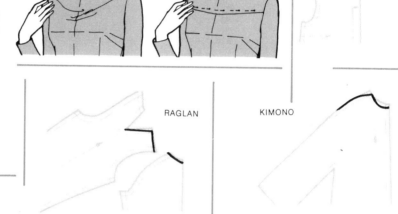

FITTED

RAGLAN

KIMONO

PRINCESS

Pigeon

When the collar and breast bones protrude, the bodice pulls above the bust and distorts the armhole seam. To correct, release the armhole seam; slash across the front above the bust and up through the center of the shoulder area to the seam. Insert strips of fabric under the slash and spread as necessary to accommodate your body contour. Keep slashed edges flat and baste securely to fabric strip. Transfer the alteration to front pattern pieces as indicated.

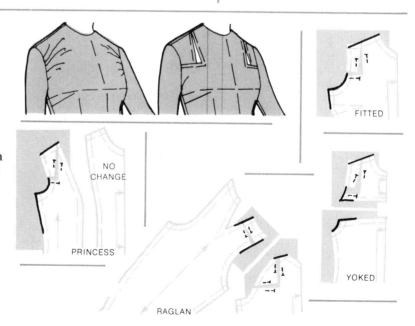

FITTED

NO CHANGE

PRINCESS

YOKED

RAGLAN

Narrow

Excess fabric appears around the armhole above the bust. This problem may be found in combination with a high, rounded back.

To correct the fitting shell, remove the sleeve and open the shoulder seam to the neck seamline. Pin a dart deep enough to remove the wrinkles. The back shoulder seam should be eased to fit the shortened front shoulder seam. Transfer the alteration to the front bodice pattern piece by slashing through the armhole and up through the center of the shoulder area. Then lap the edges to decrease the chest area. For raglan, kimono, and princess styles, take out excess fabric at the seam as indicated.

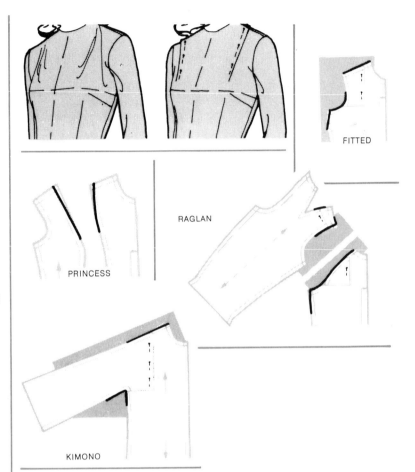

FITTED

PRINCESS

RAGLAN

KIMONO

BACK

Back alterations are needed to correct fitting problems caused by bone structure and/or posture. If your fitting shell does not mold smoothly over your body contours from the neck to the hem edge, one or more of the following alterations may be all that is needed to correct the fit. By adjusting your pattern to your circumference measurements before constructing the muslin, you have allowed the proper girth for your torso. If bone structure and posture cause further wrinkling, pulling, and uneven draping, alterations will be necessary to achieve a garment that hangs smoothly.

Very erect

This is apparent when excess fabric in the bodice back creates parallel wrinkles across the back above the shoulder blades. Corrections can accommodate your erect posture. Pin out the wrinkles, tapering to the armhole or shoulder seams at the location of the problem. Alter the bodice back pattern piece by shortening the center back length; redraw neck and shoulder edges.

Make the same alteration on raglan, kimono, and princess styles on appropriate pattern pieces.

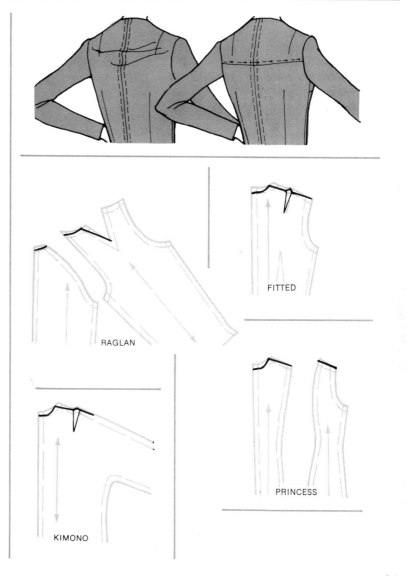

RAGLAN

FITTED

KIMONO

PRINCESS

91

Hollow shoulder blade

Excess fabric will cause vertical wrinkles between the shoulder seam and the fullest part of the shoulder blade. Your bone structure has created a hollow in this area. Release the shoulder seam. Pin a dart in the back deep enough to eliminate the wrinkles. Then ease the front shoulder seam to fit. Transfer the alterations to back bodice pattern pieces as indicated.

Make the same alteration on the back pattern pieces of raglan, kimono, and princess styles.

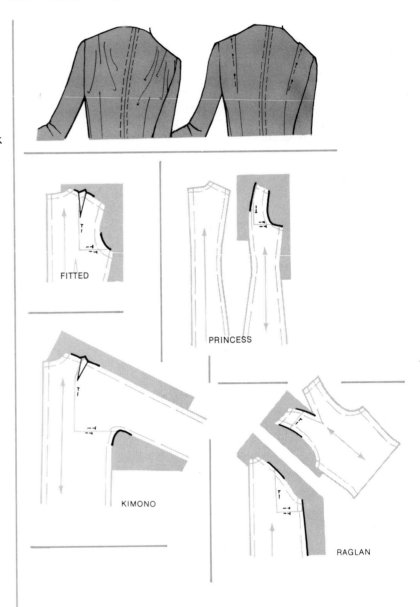

FITTED

PRINCESS

KIMONO

RAGLAN

High, rounded (dowager's hump)

Frequently a problem of mature women, this need not be a fitting difficulty. It is a figure characteristic which may be caused by extremely rounded shoulders, too. The bodice wrinkles and pulls across the shoulders and in the areas adjacent to the sleeve caps; the back length is too short. This will cause the hemline to be uneven in a jacket, or the bodice back to pull at the waist seam.

To alter your fitting shell, slash perpendicular to the grainline across the shell between the armhole seams. Release the stitching from the zipper between the slash and the neck edge. Insert strips of fabric under the slashed edges, and spread the shell the amount needed to fit properly and comfortably. Baste the strips of fabric to each half of the bodice back, keeping the slashed edges flat. Fill in the shell at the back neck edge with other fabric strips to extend the edges to the opening. Add darts to the neck edge to fit the curve of the body. Re-baste the zipper along the opening and check the fit.

To transfer the alteration to the pattern, slash the pattern horizontally as indicated, and again from the neck edge to the slash. Increase the center back length the amount needed, keeping center back seamlines aligned. Connect cutting lines and redraw shoulder dart if needed. Add a neckline dart, as indicated.

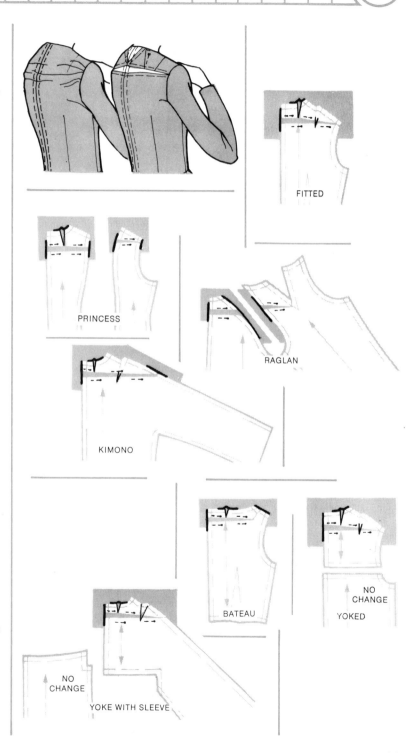

FITTED

PRINCESS

RAGLAN

KIMONO

BATEAU

NO CHANGE

YOKED

NO CHANGE

YOKE WITH SLEEVE

Narrow

Even though the bodice front has been fitted perfectly, a narrow back will cause the back of the fitting shell to be too full in the shoulder area and too loose above the waistline seam. An A-line garment may be longer at the back than at the front hemline and may hang away from the body at the shoulders and waist. To fit the garment properly, the back must be taken in to drape smoothly over the body contours.

To alter the back, pin out the excess fabric by uniting each shoulder and waistline dart in a continuous dart from shoulder to waist. To transfer the change to the fitted or A-line back pattern piece, connect the darts.

For a princess style, reduce by taking deeper side back seams.

For garments that have no back darts, slash the pattern to the shoulder seamline to eliminate excess girth. Clip the seam allowance so the pattern will lie flat (not shown). Lowered necklines and princess styles are altered as illustrated.

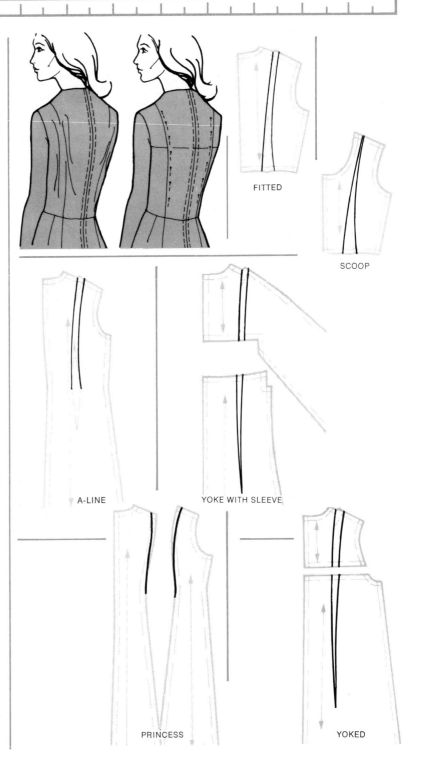

FITTED

SCOOP

A-LINE

YOKE WITH SLEEVE

PRINCESS

YOKED

Broad back or prominent shoulder blades

A broad back or prominent shoulder blades will cause the garment to pull and wrinkle across the widest area of the back. The fabric binds, and the absence of wearing ease makes it difficult to raise your arms. The strain at the armhole seam could be enough to break the threads unless the back is altered.

To correct, release the stitching at the shoulder seams, shoulder darts, and side seams. At the most curved area, slash across the back of your fitting shell perpendicular to the lengthwise grain. Then slash up to the point of the dart, parallel to the grain. Continue the slash through the center of the dart. Insert strips of fabric under the slashed edges and spread the amount needed; baste the strips in place. Shape the dart to fit the body contour; restitch the seam. Try on the shell and test: raise your arms to check fit and wearing ease. To transfer the alteration to the back pattern piece, redraw the dart. For other styles, alter back pattern pieces as illustrated, adding shoulder darts if none exist.

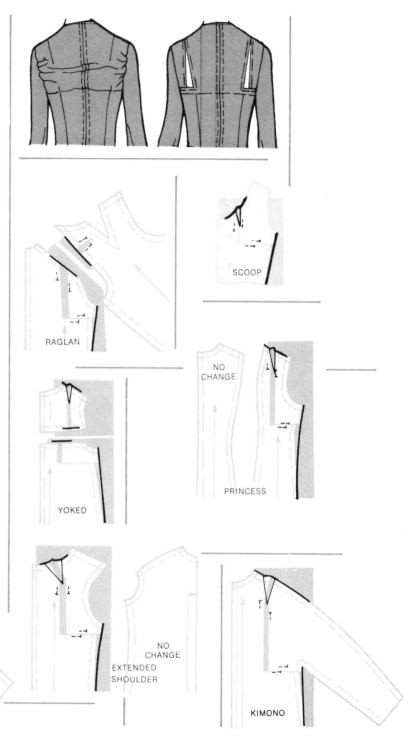

RAGLAN

SCOOP

YOKED

NO CHANGE

PRINCESS

YOKE WITH SLEEVE

NO CHANGE EXTENDED SHOULDER

KIMONO

Swayback

A smooth, even line will be interrupted by wrinkles across the back below the waistline in a figure with a swayback caused by body contour or posture. To alter the fitting shell, pin out the excess fabric, tapering the fold to the side seams. On the pattern, shorten the center back the same amount. Redraw the cutting line, and redraw and shorten the darts as shown.

Shorten the center back of A-line and princess styles as indicated. Because the skirt portion will be shifted off grain by this correction, you must redraw the grainline. Also, redraw the lower part of the dart, shortening it to fit your contours.

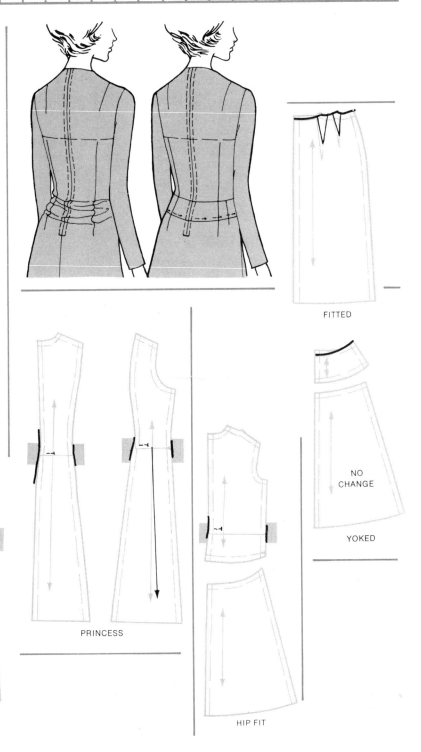

FITTED

NO CHANGE

YOKED

A-LINE

PRINCESS

HIP FIT

HIPS

The basic circumference adjustments have allowed for adequate girth in the hip area of your fitting shell. However, there remain several figure variations around the hips which may require more extensive fitting than can be provided by circumference adjustments alone. Bone structure, posture, and excess flesh affect hip fit. To be flattering, a garment should drape smoothly and evenly across the hip, buttocks, and upper thigh areas. Be particularly alert to your fitting needs throughout the hip area in a fitted garment.

You will find that the hip area is comparatively easy to fit, so do not hestitate to experiment with your fitting shell to achieve perfect and personalized fit.

Protruding pelvic bones

Any garment designed to closely fit body contours will reveal protruding pelvic bones. The front pulls between the pelvic bones and the bone structure is visually emphasized rather than blended into the figure.

To correct the fit, release the stitching from the front darts and waist seam. Position the darts to make the fitting shell fit smoothly over the pelvic bones; reshape the darts as needed. Transfer the alteration to the front pattern piece. If this has reduced the waistline circumference, add this amount to the side seams.

The alteration is not usually needed in A-line styles. To alter a fitted princess style, adapt the side and side front seams to fit; add darts if necessary. Alter skirts with fitted yokes as indicated.

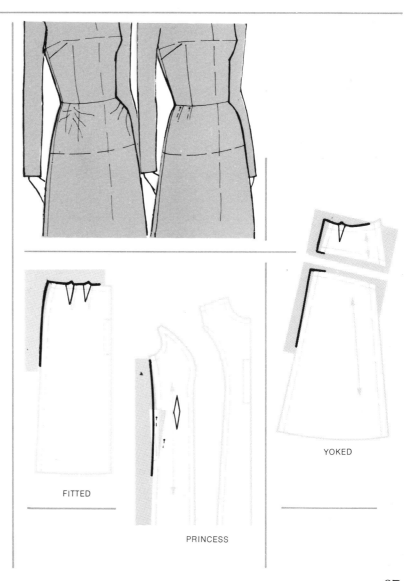

FITTED

PRINCESS

YOKED

97

One large hip

All figures are slightly asymmetrical, and a special alteration is needed only when the garment appears to be distorted. One large hip will exaggerate the fit and cause an uneven hemline. Also, the skirt will pull up on both the front and back sides of the large hip. In some styles this may not be evident, but in a fitted garment it is of great significance.

To alter a fitting shell with a waist seam, release the darts, and the waist and side seams where the large hip protrudes. Lower the skirt until the grainlines and hem are straight. Insert strips of fabric at the sides and waist; baste. Pin darts to fit. For an A-line garment, release the side seam and back dart on the shorter side. Insert fabric strips, spread the amount needed, and baste in place. Pin the back dart to fit the shape of the body.

To transfer this alteration to your pattern pieces, you must make an exact tracing of the front and back pattern pieces—you will then enlarge half the pattern and leave the other half unchanged. Transfer the alteration to the side needed (illustrations show the right hip altered).

For princess styles, adapt the method used for A-line styles.

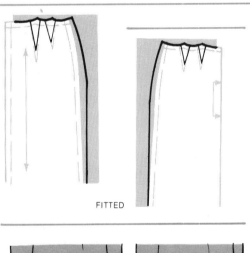

FITTED

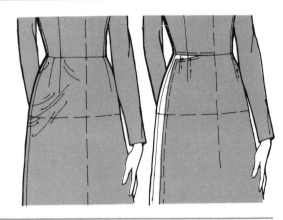

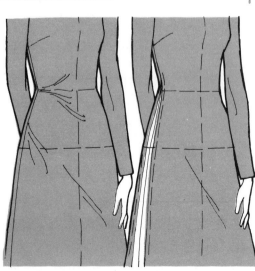

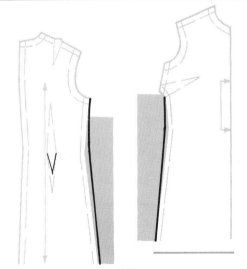

A-LINE

98

Flat buttocks

The fitting shell hangs in loose wrinkles and collapses over flat buttocks. Because the garment allows for fullness not present, the hem will hang lower in the back than in the front. To fit, release the stitching in the waist and back darts. Pin the darts to the shape of the body. To even the hemline, pin out excess fabric the length of the skirt and across the hipline as shown. To transfer the alteration to the back pattern piece, redraw the darts, then pin a tuck the amount needed parallel to the grainline. Shorten the center back length the same amount that was decreased horizontally. On an A-line garment, remove the stitching from the zipper below the back bustline markings. Release the back darts and pin them to fit; they can be shorter and narrower. To preserve the waist circumference, reduce it at the center back and side seams.

For a princess style, reduce at the side, side back, and center back seam to fit. For yoke-seamed skirts, alter as indicated.

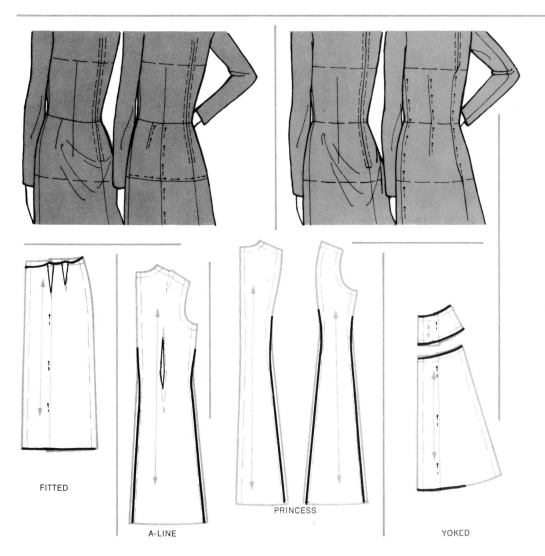

FITTED

A-LINE

PRINCESS

YOKED

Large buttocks

Excess flesh creates wrinkles between the waistline and hipline; the fabric is pulled and the side seams are strained. The garment is shorter at the back hemline than at the front. To correct a fitted garment with a waist seam, release the skirt darts and the waist seam. Pin the darts to fit smoothly, shortening and widening them. Add to the side seams the amount reduced from the waist circumference by widening the darts. Add to the center back length to even the hemline, if necessary. Alter the pattern as illustrated.

For an A-line style, remove the stitching from the zipper below the back bustline marking, back darts, side seams, and center back seam. Add strips of fabric, spread the amount needed, and baste. Pin the darts to fit. Transfer the alteration to the pattern, as shown.

For a princess style and yoked-seam skirts, alter back pattern pieces as indicated.

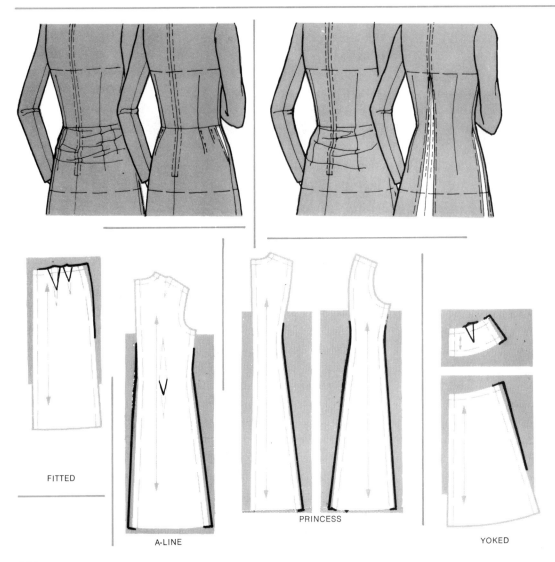

FITTED

A-LINE

PRINCESS

YOKED

Thigh bulge

No matter how small or large a woman's figure, fit may be distorted by thigh bulge. On a fitted garment, the skirt pulls and wrinkles at the upper thigh just below the hipline. It may not be noticeable in loosely fitted styles. Hip circumference is not affected by heavy thighs in this problem.

To correct the fitting shell, release the side seam to the hipline. Add strips of fabric to the shell, spread to fit, and baste the strips in place. Transfer one-fourth of the amount needed for the alteration to the front pattern piece; slash at the same point on the side seam, then down to the hem, paralleling the grainline. Draw new cutting lines. Alter the back pattern piece the same amount.

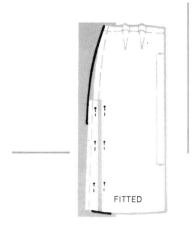

FITTED

ABDOMEN

Adjusting the circumference of your pattern has provided you
with the necessary girth in the abdomen area, but alterations may
be required to accommodate your body contour.

Large

A large abdomen will affect the
hang of your skirt, causing it to
ride up in front and the side
seams to pull forward. For garments with a waist seam,
release the front waist seam
and darts. Drop the skirt front
until it hangs evenly. Insert a
fabric strip and baste it to the
top of the skirt. Pin the darts to
fit your contour. If this alteration makes the waistline
smaller, add the necessary
amount to the side seams.
Stitch darts and seams and
check the fit again. Transfer the
alteration to the pattern piece,
lengthening the center front as
needed and redrawing darts
according to your contours.

An A-line garment is altered
by slashing the front up to the
bust area. Insert fabric strips
and spread the edges the
amount necessary for side
seams, waistline, and hipline
to fall into position. Baste fabric
strips to the slashed edges.
Transfer the alteration to the
pattern front, slashing through
the bust dart to make the pattern lie flat; allow edges to
overlap.

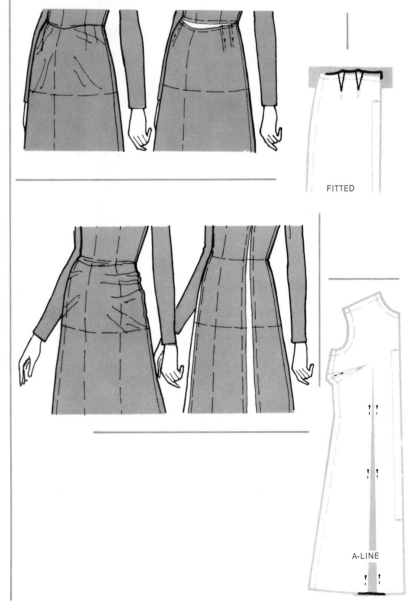

FITTED

A-LINE

Flat

A flat abdomen also affects the hang of the skirt; the hem is uneven due to the wrinkling of excess fabric through this area. The garment allows length not needed by your figure. To correct garments with a waist seam, pin out excess fabric between the waist and hipline until the hem edge is even. Taper the fold at the side seams. Transfer the alteration to the front pattern piece, reshaping darts and decreasing center front length.

For A-line garments, pin out excess fabric in the form of a doublepointed dart which extends from the bust to the hip level.

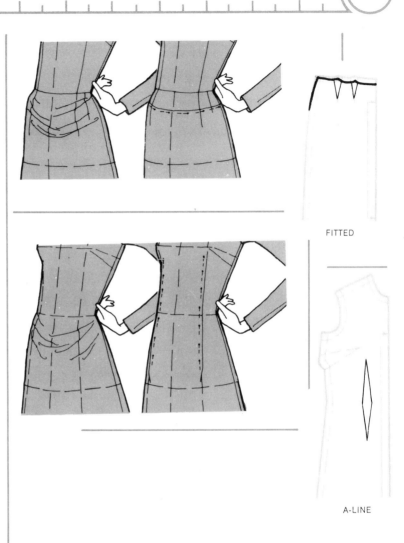

FITTED

A-LINE

103

The Permanent Pattern

The greatest value of the adjustments and alterations you have made lies in their being repeatedly used to build fit into each fashion project you undertake. The variations between your figure and the standard will probably remain relatively constant. Barring any changes in your body due to weight loss or gain or to re-proportioning, a permanent record of your figure and its fitting requirements—in effect, a permanent pattern—will be a priceless sewing tool to use again and again.

Having arrived at this point in the creation of perfectly fitted clothes, it only remains for you to refine fit in terms of each fashion design and fabric you choose. The adjustments and alterations which you have found to be necessary are your general rules of thumb in establishing fit. The reaction of an individual fabric to a design and your figure cannot be accounted for in adjustments and alterations. Your ultimate success in creating clothes that fit perfectly depends on combining pattern adjustments and alterations with the interpretation of fit in any fashion fabric you might select.

Through the course of this book you may have made the necessary pattern adjustments in a fitting shell. Having altered it to fit your individual contours, you must then transfer both adjustments and alterations directly to your basic pattern pieces. The result is a pattern with a personalized fit which can be used in adapting other styles to your individual frame and contours. Your original tissue pattern pieces may, after being adjusted and altered, need some support to function effectively as a master pattern throughout your many sewing ventures.

It is advisable to try on your fitting shell periodically to check its fit. If your weight or contours change, use your shell as a gauge, and make further alterations in it to keep your permanent pattern up to date. Its use will facilitate and professionalize the fitting and construction of every garment you choose to make, and you will have assurance of achieving superb results before you begin. On the following pages, you will find information pertinent to the use of your fitting shell as a valuable sewing tool.

MAKING A PERMANENT PATTERN

Once your fitting shell has been adjusted to your satisfaction, you are ready to create some form of permanent record of the adjustments. Preserving the work you have done is one of the most important steps you can take. Your permanent pattern will include, in its most useful form, all the fitting knowledge you have gained about your figure.

If you use the Vogue Professional Fitting Program #1001 for your fitting shell, you have a permanent master pattern when you complete your adjustments and alterations.

If you use the Vogue Basic Fitting Shell #1004, you should make a permanent pattern from your adjusted tissue pattern using one of the following procedures.

First, carefully check all the changes you have made from the beginning of the fitting process, combining any that were made at different stages in the same area of the garment. If you kept accurate notes throughout, this will be an easy task. If you are uncertain about the changes in any area, measure the fitting shell and compare it to your pattern tissue.

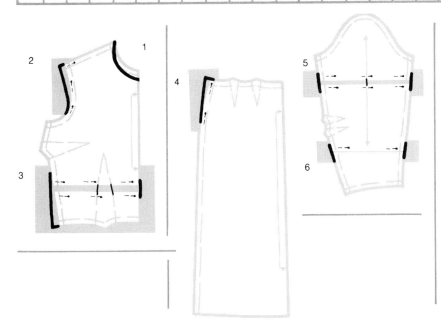

1 LOWER NECKLINE ½" (13mm)
2 EXTEND SHOULDERS ⅜" (10mm)
3 LENGTHEN BODICE ¾" (20mm)
4 INCREASE WAISTLINE 1" (25mm)
5 LENGTHEN UPPER ARM ¾" (20mm)
6 SHORTEN LOWER ARM ½" (13mm)

Record all of your changes right on the pattern tissue. Here are a few tips to help you simplify this procedure.

☐ Use different colored pens to indicate changes—one for basic length adjustments, one for basic circumference adjustments, and another for any special alterations you need to custom-fit your garments.

☐ Mark the exact amount of each change clearly. Use a + to denote increases and a − to denote decreases.

☐ Label any asymmetrical alterations as to whether they are for the right or left side. Your permanent pattern should maintain the cutting line for the larger side. Mark the stitching line for each side with contrasting colors and indicate which one is right and which one is left.

☐ If your pattern is badly mangled as a result of a series of adjustments in an effort to perfect the fit, either trace the entire pattern onto transparent non-woven fabric (see page 106), or purchase a new tissue pattern to adjust and mark up. If your pattern has a multitude of unnecessary slashes and/or corrections, it will be too confusing to be an effective fitting tool.

Once you have transferred every change to your new pattern, you are ready to make the pattern permanent in one of two ways: you can back the tissue pattern with an iron-on non-woven interfacing, or you can trace the pattern onto a transparent non-woven fabric. Products made especially for this purpose are sold in the sewing notions or interfacing section of fabric stores or departments.

After the pattern has been backed or traced, roll it around a large cardboard cylinder to store. Place it printed side out so the pattern will curl the right way when unrolled. Folding or creasing the pattern will subject it to unnecessary wear and tear.

Fusing the pattern

To make your master pattern durable and to keep your original adjustments and alterations visible, use an iron-on non-woven interfacing as a stable backing. First press the pattern pieces to remove wrinkles and to make sure they are flat.

To attach the interfacing to the pattern pieces, use a warm dry iron, and work on a large padded surface. Place each pattern piece printed side down, on tissue paper, then place the adhesive side of the interfacing on the wrong side of each pattern piece. Use weights to hold the pattern pieces and interfacing in place. Arrange the pattern pieces under the interfacing carefully.

On the right side of the interfacing, press from the center and work toward the edges until the entire surface of the fabric has been fused to each pattern piece. Avoid creating wrinkles as you fuse; a tiny wrinkle can cause serious distortion in your carefully prepared permanent pattern. Let the pattern pieces cool, then cut them out.

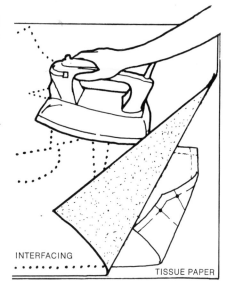

INTERFACING

TISSUE PAPER

Tracing the pattern

Use a ball point or felt-tip pen that does not smudge; it may be helpful to use different colors for the cutting lines, grainlines, and seamlines. Make all lines heavy enough to be seen easily, as you will be placing fashion patterns on top of your permanent pattern pieces to evaluate the design ease and wearing ease.

You will need a large flat surface on which to work. Place a large sheet of white paper under the pattern pieces so the lines will be easier to see. Make sure your pattern is free of wrinkles. Do not use pins to anchor the pattern pieces, as the lines will be distorted; instead use paperweights. As you trace, use your French curve, T-square, yardstick, and see-through ruler to help in duplicating the pattern line for line.

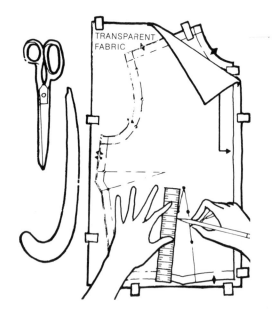

TRANSPARENT FABRIC

USING YOUR PERMANENT PATTERN

The purpose of making a permanent pattern is to create a personalized fitting tool. Having made the fitting shell, you may have learned that a few simple adjustments will solve many problems, and you can apply them to any design you make. If, however, you need to do more to perfect the adjustments in a fashion pattern, learn to use your master pattern as a guideline for all other designs.

Aligning the patterns

Your permanent pattern represents your body contours plus enough wearing ease for a comfortable and flattering fit. It also represents the minimum amounts of ease with which you should be cutting your fashion garments.

To use your permanent pattern with fashion patterns, place the permanent pattern under the corresponding pieces of the fashion pattern. Align the fashion pattern with your permanent pattern at the shoulders of a bodice or a dress and at the waistline of a skirt or pants. Compare and determine all the necessary length adjustments from these positions. Take into consideration any design ease that has been built into the length, such as with a blouson top. This information would be printed right on the tissue of your fashion pattern.

Next, align the fashion pattern and your permanent pattern at the waistlines and determine all necessary circumference adjustments. Once again, take into consideration the design ease built into each area of the garment.

Other specialized alterations, such as square shoulders or a swayback, should be handled at this time as well.

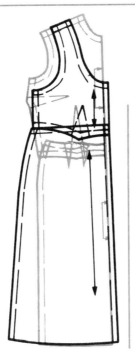

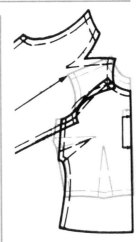

It is essential that you have a clear understanding of wearing ease and design ease before you even begin to evaluate adjustment needs. You may want to review this information on pages 33–34.

All fashion designs originate from a basic pattern like this one. It may be helpful to view your permanent pattern as the basic pattern for each new garment you plan to sew. The difference is that your individual proportions have been incorporated into this master pattern and any designs originating from it are therefore created especially for you.

Your permanent pattern includes all the information regarding your shape and how it differs from the standard proportions for which the pattern was designed—information that has been translated into workable figures and logged right on your master pattern. Use these figures as you analyze the fashion design you are about to make.

Locate all major pattern pieces and the key positions on each: bust, waist, shoulder, etc. Designs that have underlays, foldbacks, side insets, etc. should be positioned so that you have a clear image of the garment and how the pieces go together.

The necessary modifications can be determined in one of two ways. You can compare the figures that represent your variations from the standard, or you can align the fashion pattern with the permanent pattern and compare the fit.

Comparing the figures

The amount of each adjustment reflects how the measurements in your permanent pattern differ from the standards. These figures can be used as a guide to determining the necessary adjustments at corresponding areas on the fashion design. In most cases you can automatically make the adjustments and proceed with the sewing process. Sometimes it is possible to avoid an adjustment altogether, such as with a design where there is no waistline fitting: a waistline adjustment in this situation would be ineffective and unnecessary. The same would be true with styles that have great amounts of design ease: the fact that your hips are 1" (25mm) smaller or 1" (25mm) larger than the standard really becomes unimportant in a smock or tent design.

Use your common sense, fitting knowledge, and good judgment as you determine when and when not to make an adjustment.

5 Refining the Fit

The time has come to get the first glimpse of how your new garment is going to look on you and to see how your fashion fabric adapts to the style you have chosen. You will also take the final step toward personalizing your fit. Since you have already incorporated all the necessary adjustments into the pattern before you cut the fashion fabric, the alterations you make here should be minimal.

The choice of fabric, any special design elements, and the construction techniques you used will all have an influence on the final fit of your garment. This is your opportunity to adjust to those influences and refine your fit to perfection.

It is extremely important to wear proper undergarments when fitting your garment. They should fit well—not so tightly that they cause bulges—and should suit the style of the garment. Check to see that your bra straps are adjusted correctly and that your bustline is neither too low nor too high. Once you have determined the correct and most comfortable position, do not change it; doing so would affect the placement of the bust darts or shaping and perhaps ruin the fit of your garment.

Shoes with heels affect the distribution of body weight by shifting your center of balance. This changes the contours of your legs and torso, and affects your manner of walking. Different heel heights will necessitate slight differences in fit and hem length. Choose a shoe that enhances the look of your garment. If you have not yet purchased the shoes you'll be wearing, wear a pair similar in style and heel height throughout the fitting process.

Fashions that will be worn with a belt should be fitted with a belt. Any other accessories that would affect fit should also be worn when fitting the garment.

Basting the Garment

Pin basting, hand basting, or machine basting can be used to join your garment sections for the first fitting. Each method has its advantages; the fabric and/or your personal choice will determine which to use. In any event, the first fitting should include only the sections that constitute the basic garment shell; omit collars, cuffs, waistbands, facings, sleeves, and any details such as pockets and trims. Baste darts, pleats, and tucks and pin or baste all major seams. Press the seams open lightly with your fingers.

Pin basting

Join garment sections, wrong sides together, with the fabric sections right side out. Pin along the seamlines parallel to the cut edge every 2" to 3" (5cm to 7.5cm). In curved areas you may have to pin a bit closer. Catch only a small amount of fabric with each pin to avoid puckers. For set-in sleeves, place pins perpendicular to the cut edge.

Pin basting is not satisfactory for heavy, thick fabrics, vinyls, leathers, or fabrics that mar easily. Use hand or machine basting for garment areas that are intricate or require greater control and stability.

Hand basting

Join garment sections, right sides together, with even basting stitches. Silk thread is preferable for fabrics that mar because it will not leave marks as readily as cotton or synthetic thread.

If your fabric design must be matched, fold one edge along the seamline, match it to the opposite seamline, and slip baste it from the right side.

With metallics, beaded fabric, or bulky fabric, lap the edges to match the seamlines and join using even or diagonal basting stitches.

Machine basting

Machine basting can be used for fabrics that are not easily marred or when only a minimum of fitting is anticipated. The procedure is the same as for hand basting. Use a long machine stitch that can be removed easily for changes.

Closing the Open Edge

How you get into and out of your garment depends upon the type of closure. Match the closure area accurately once you have the garment on your body. A friend can be a helpful and sometimes necessary aid at this point.

Lapped edges

Closures that lap can be found at various positions on a garment. Thread-trace the center or placement markings, baste any interfacing in place, and fold back any extended facings before you begin fitting.

Match the center or placement markings and place pins perpendicular to the markings at areas of stress such as the neck, bust, waist, and hips. Position any additional pins needed to keep the garment in place during the fitting.

In-seam closures

To fit a garment that will be closed along the seamline with a zipper, snaps, hook and loop fastener, etc., pin securely along the seamline. Fold one edge along the seamline, match the fold to the seamline of the opposite edge, and pin perpendicular to the seamline for a smooth fit. Position enough pins so the closure area will not come apart during the fitting. If the closure is in the back, you will need help securing the pins.

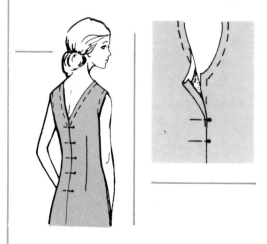

112

Edges that meet

Garment edges that meet and do not overlap ultimately will be secured by loops and buttons, buckles, or ties, if they do not hang unfastened.

Baste any interfacing in place. For edges with an applied facing, match the edges at the seamlines and pin them together at areas of stress with enough additional pins to keep the garment in place throughout the fitting. For edges with an extended facing, fold along the foldline and pin the facing in place. Baste a strip of seam binding or twill tape to one folded edge and pin the corresponding edge to it with folds meeting. Position enough pins to keep the garment in place throughout the fitting.

Asymmetrical edges

Edges that fall on angles within the garment need to be positioned properly for an accurate fit. In a wrap garment the overlap is large and often cut at an angle. The resulting edge is on the bias and will stretch; take care not to overhandle it. First pin the garment together along the placement or center markings, placing pins perpendicular to the markings. Position additional pins on each side to hold the extensions in place throughout the fitting.

Making Changes

Any alterations you need to make must be done with care and forethought. Begin with changes at the shoulder and work down to the hem. Remember that garment sections are interrelated: a change in one area may affect the fit in another area.

Wider seam allowances

Heavy, thick, firm, and textured fabrics will often need wider seam allowances simply because more of the seam allowance is taken up in the bulk of the seam. Also, these fabrics have less drape, and thus closely fitted areas may need additional circumference to fit smoothly. Make the vertical seam allowances approximately 1" to 1½" (25mm to 3.8cm) wide when cutting out your fabric so you will have that extra pinch that might be needed to mold the fabric to your body.

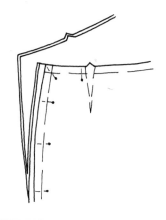

Releasing seam allowances

During a fitting it is sometimes necessary to release a seam allowance to make an accurate evaluation of the fit. This must be done with caution to avoid trouble later, when you are sewing your garment together. Staystitch along the seamline first and clip the seam allowance only at the point of strain; avoid clipping into the seamline. If you find one clip does not relieve the strain, make a few additional clips at even intervals on each side of the first. Clips made thoughtlessly will prohibit an exact fit if you find that a seamline needs to be raised or let out slightly.

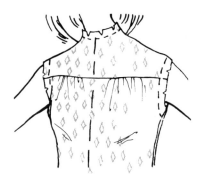

Marking changes

You can pin or baste changes into position, you can mark them with pins or chalk, or you can pin out excess fabric along the seams and then make the changes after the garment has been removed. The method you use is determined by the fabric and the type of alteration.

To pin or baste the changes at the seamline, turn in one edge the amount of the change and match the fold to the corrected seamline. Slip baste or pin together at right angles along the seamline.

Use tailor's chalk or pins to mark surface changes such as new seamlines at the neck, armhole, or bust points as well as placement lines for pockets and trims. After fitting, thread trace markings.

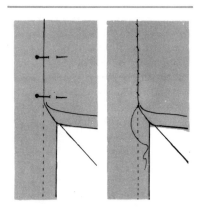

You can also remove the basting while you still have the garment on and pin the altered seamline or dart with the seam allowances on the outside. Remove the garment, chalk-mark the altered seamlines on the wrong side along the pins, baste along the corrected seamline, and fit again.

To reposition a dart, release the basting and reshape or reposition by pinning the two layers together along the new stitching lines. Remove the garment, turn it to the wrong side and mark the fabric with chalk along the pins. Remove the pins, rebaste the dart from the inside of the garment and fit again.

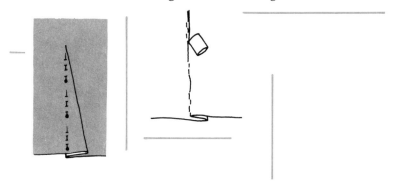

If you need to remove excess fabric in situations such as a swayback or sloping shoulders, pin the folds of fabric next to the seamline to achieve a proper fit. Remove the garment, measure the amount of the alteration, and transfer the alteration to the appropriate seamline, dart or garment area.

Evaluating the Fit

The ultimate goal of all the attention we are giving to pattern adjustments and alterations is a personalized fashion wardrobe that is comfortable, flattering, and beautifully constructed. To achieve this you must understand your figure, your preferences, and the fundamentals of good fit . . . you must be able to evaluate fit so that you can perfect the fit of each fashion garment you make.

Understanding the basic components—comfort, appearance, and structure—is essential before you proceed with the basic refinement alterations of the garment shell and each specific design feature.

COMFORT

Comfort is of primary importance for a perfectly fitted garment. However beautifully designed and constructed, a garment will hang in your closet untouched if it isn't comfortable to wear.

Regardless of the design, you should be able to move without strain or restriction. Sit, bend, walk, and move your arms as you evaluate how the garment feels. If the design will be worn in unusual situations such as swimming, jogging, or other active sports, move in a manner similar to that for which it will be worn.

A garment should always return to its original position on your body when movement ceases. If it is necessary to pull or tug at the fabric in order to have it return, the garment is too tight and comfort will be diminished. On the other hand, if the garment is too loose and is constantly falling off your shoulders or hanging low at the waist, the annoyance of the improper fit will also limit comfort considerably.

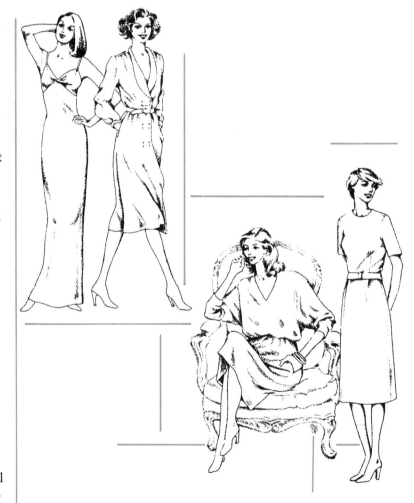

APPEARANCE

The relationship of the design lines to your body must be taken into consideration when evaluating fit. It is most important to consider proportion in the initial stages of fabric and pattern selection, of course, but additional refining can be done at this point to ensure a flattering appearance. Fabric style and color can have a great effect on the visual proportions of your finished garment, so evaluate them with a critical eye.

A figure which is broad in the hip area may find it unflattering to wear a garment with a horizontal seam that falls directly at the widest part of the hips. On the other hand, a figure with narrow hips may welcome that horizontal line to create more flattering proportions.

Contrasting colors or obvious seaming that divide the figure horizontally must be evaluated carefully to ensure that the lines fall at a flattering point on the body.

Accents and trims should be kept in scale with the figure. A short-waisted figure may look chunky with a waistband that is too wide. A narrower band would be much more flattering.

A petite figure may be overwhelmed by a huge collar. Proportion it by narrowing it from the outside edges. You can create a more pleasing proportion without changing the design of the garment.

A garment should hang smoothly from your shoulders. The design will indicate how close to your body it should be. Loose-fitting garments may be designed with much excess fullness, as in a cape, tunic top, gathered skirt, or large billowing sleeves. Close-fitting or fitted garments will conform to the body contours, as in a slim skirt, shaped sleeves or body-hugging swimwear.

Regardless of the design, the garment should be free from wrinkles, sags, and strain. Any unwanted lines created while the garment is on your body are the result of poor posture or poor fit. If posture is the cause and it is uncorrectable, a fitting refinement is needed. Your goal is to achieve an overall pleasing appearance, altering to remove any unwanted wrinkles—but be cautious not to overfit, which only accentuates the problem.

Horizontal wrinkles are a sure indication that the garment is too tight or that the proportion is wrong. Correct it with a circumference alteration or adjust the proportion as necessary.

Sagging vertical lines that are not part of the design may be a sign that the garment is too big. Correct this with a circumference alteration.

Pulls in the neck and shoulder area are a result of strain and an indication that the neck is too tight or the shoulders too narrow. Correct with an appropriate alteration.

In order to remedy each situation, you will need to determine the cause. Find the point from which the wrinkles originate and then you can decide what refinements are needed to make the correction. Pages 125–141 provide specific information on the cause, effect, and solution of a range of fitting abnormalities; use these pages as an encyclopedia as you evaluate your fit, determine the cause of any undesirable effects, and prepare to correct them.

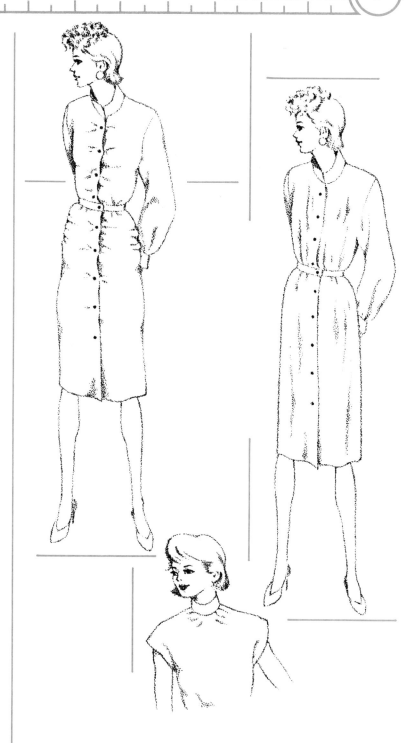

STRUCTURE

Accurate seamlines and proper grainlines are crucial to a well-fitted garment. Horizontal seams should be parallel to the floor. Uneven seams may be an indication of figure characteristics such as one high shoulder or hip, or one side of the body being fuller than the other. Determine the cause and correct accordingly, but remember not to over alter the garment which may then emphasize the figure characteristic you are trying to camouflage or deemphasize. Consider other solutions that would change the body line, such as the use of one shoulder pad to lift the garment and even it out rather than altering the garment. Vertical seams should fall perpendicular to the floor. Seams that swing away from this line (unless designed to do so) must be altered to achieve a perfect fit and visual appeal. This discrepancy is most often corrected at a horizontal seam such as the waistline or shoulders. Determine the cause and correct accordingly.

Most fashions are designed on the lengthwise grain for a more stable and durable garment. Grainline that is not perpendicular to the floor (unless otherwise intended) will create a garment that is both visually and structurally distorted; it will tend to twist or sag as it hangs. Care must be taken at the very beginning stages of construction to achieve and maintain the perfect grain of your fabric and garment.

When fitting, look for grain distortion indicated by wrinkles, sagging, or twisting. The lengthwise seams should be perpendicular to the floor and the crosswise seams should be parallel to the floor, unless designed otherwise.

Grainline that has become distorted could be the result of poor construction and must be corrected before you can continue the fitting. If the distortion is the result of a specific figure characteristic, an alteration is needed. Determine the cause and correct accordingly.

Bias-cut garments must be handled with care to avoid stretching. They should drape and mold to your body without unwanted pulls and sags. Always allow a bias-cut garment to hang for 24 hours before you complete your final fitting. The fabric will stretch and the garment will assume a slightly different shape from when you first sewed it together.

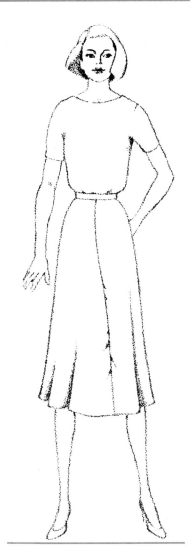

Fitting Checklist

By carefully fitting each area of your garment you will create the dimensions needed to flatter your figure, the fabric, and the fashion design. You now understand the basics of pattern adjustments and how to proceed with a fitting, as well as the elements of a well-fitted garment. The following checklist of fitting standards will help you evaluate your garment as you strive for the perfect fit.

□ Vertical seams are perpendicular to the floor.

□ Horizontal seams are parallel to the floor.

□ Shoulder seams rest smoothly on the top of the shoulder and end at the shoulder joint.

□ Armhole seams create a smooth curve around the arm with sleeve caps free of puckers.

□ Necklines fall close to the body without pulling or gaping and are free of strain.

□ Bust darts point to the fullest part of the bust. All other darts point to the fullest part of the body contour over which they are shaped.

□ Waistline seams fall at the natural waist. Waistbands are snug but comfortable.

□ Cuffs end at the wrist bone.

□ Hems are even, parallel to the floor, and a flattering length.

□ Garment fits smoothly around the body, with no pulls or wrinkles.

□ Garment is comfortable to wear.

121

SPECIAL FABRICS

Giving a fabric the special attention it needs by fitting, as well as when constructing the garment, can make a world of difference in the final product. A bit of knowledge regarding the fitting characteristics of special fabrics and a few handy techniques can turn a possible frustration into a simple pleasure.

In some cases the use of these fabrics represents a considerable investment in time and money. You may want to consider making a fitting shell if the design also involves special fitting considerations.

Fabrics with give

Knits, and stretch wovens all have built-in stretchability ranging from the maximum stretch needed for active sportswear to minimum stretch used for shape retention. It's important to consider the amount of stretch and recovery in these fabrics when choosing a pattern, since it will obviously affect the fit of the garment. Some stretch fabrics can be handled just like any stable fabric and should be altered accordingly. Others, such as those used for swimwear or body-hugging evening wear, require special fitting techniques. Patterns labeled "For Stretchable Knits Only" are designed to make use of the stretchability of the fabric for comfort and mobility; they have little or no ease built into them.

Make any of the flat pattern adjustments you would normally make on any other pattern. Baste the seams and alter accordingly.

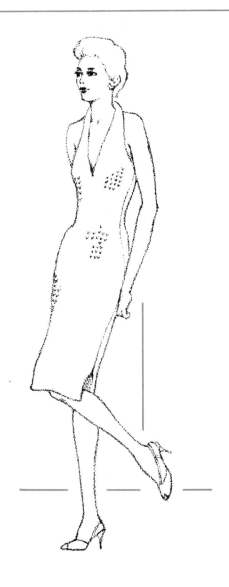

Fabrics with luster

Satin, taffeta, brocade, metallic, beaded, and sequined fabrics require a knowledge of their nature rather than special techniques.

Make your normal adjustments. If the fabric is fragile or if fitting changes could leave permanent marks, you may want to make a test garment first. In any event, baste and alter with care to avoid marking the fabric.

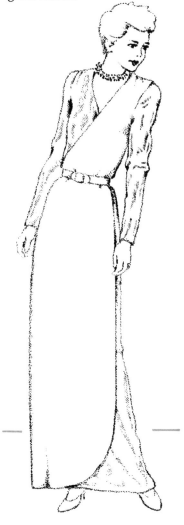

Fabrics with surface style

Napped or pile fabrics such as corduroy, velvet, velveteen, velour and melton all require some special considerations before cutting. Make any flat pattern adjustments you normally make. If the fabric is bulky, it is wise to cut wider seam allowances for any additional alterations.

These fabrics will not drape like others. You may find it necessary to remove excess fullness in order to achieve a flattering fit. Follow all the normal procedures for alterations, keeping in mind that the final result should be comfortable and flattering.

Suede, leather and leather-like fabrics

Leather, suede, vinyl, and ciré, with their luxurious beauty, are available in many weights, styles, and colors. For best results select a skin or fabric that has some drapability and select a pattern design with simple lines. Avoid styles that require extensive easing because leathers, suedes and leather-like fabrics do not ease well.

Make all the standard adjustments you would normally make. Cut wider seam allowances on the vertical seams in close-fitting areas of the garment; since the fabric does not give, you may decide you need some extra circumference for comfort.

Fabrics that flow and float

Sheers, lace, and crepe de chine are supple, drapable fabrics that glide and flow on your body. Complete your usual pattern adjustments and fit for final refinements. Sheer and lace fabrics should not be fitted tightly, as the tenuous nature of the fabric may not endure stress.

For a flattering fit, it can be helpful to make a separate camisole in a smooth, lightweight coordinating fabric, to wear under the fashion garment. The separate garment allows the fashion garment to flow and float without restrictions from body moisture, static, or undergarments.

Fabrics with a special design

Plaids, stripes, border prints and large design motifs require some attention before you cut the fabric.

Make any flat pattern adjustments you normally make. With plaids, horizontal stripes and border prints, the exact hem length must be determined before you cut your fabric. Judge the length from another similarly styled garment, measure the length and adjust the pattern accordingly. Position the hemline on the fabric so that the design is strategically placed. The same procedure should be followed for sleeve length on these prints.

With any other alterations you must make, consider the consequences of the design. If it will distort the design in such a manner that you will ruin the beauty of the fabric, consider other alternatives. Proper pattern selection is extremely important with these fabrics.

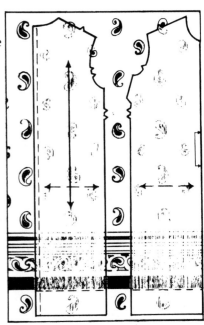

Fashion Fabric Alterations

Now that your garment has taken shape in the fabric of your
choice, you may find the need for minor alterations as you strive
to perfect the fit. If you made a basic fitting shell, any further
attention to fit should be minimal, but as you translate your adjustments to specific designs and fabrics, you may find the
alterations in this section helpful. If you did not make a basic
fitting shell, these alterations are made after your pattern tissue
adjustments have been made and your garment has been cut and
basted.

   The changes in this section are made directly on your fashion
fabric, unlike those in Chapter 4, which are techniques used for a
basic fitting shell, which often require slashing into the garment.

THE SHOULDER AREA

On your shoulders rest the balance and weight of the entire garment; it is essential that the shoulder area fit properly. The seam
of a regular shoulder line should rest on top of the shoulder and
extend from the base of the neck to the arm hinge. The fit of an
extended or dropped shoulder line depends on the styling of a
specific design; the shoulder line will extend beyond the edge of
the shoulder bone. When the shoulder seam has been adjusted to
your personal contours, the fit of the armhole and sleeve may be
affected. Raglan and kimono sleeve styles involve specific fitting
techniques, which are described on pages 132 and 133.

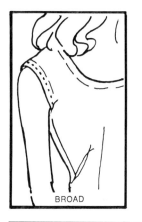

   It is customary to begin fitting in the shoulder area, for any
minor corrections made here will affect the fit and balance of the
entire garment. For any shoulder changes, take into account fabric weight and wearing ease. The shoulder and armhole areas
must have enough ease comfort for motion.

   To adjust the width for broad shoulders, re-mark the armhole
seamline, extending it into the seam allowance as much as necessary at the top and tapering to the original seamline at the
underarm. You must make this alteration before doing any clipping at the armhole; otherwise it will be impossible to extend the
seamline.

   To decrease the shoulder width for narrow shoulders, re-mark
the seamline, taking a larger seam allowance at the top and tapering to the original seamline at the underarm. Remember, a little
bit goes a long way on this alteration, so do not overfit.

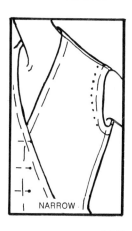

To further adjust the angle for sloping shoulders, pin in excess fabric along the shoulder, tapering to the neck seamline. Drop the lower armhole seamline the same amount; re-mark. If your garment will accommodate shoulder pads, these may correct sloping shoulders.

To give yourself more armhole circumference for square shoulders, let out the shoulder seam at the edge of the armhole, tapering it to the neck seamline. Raise the armhole seamline at the underarm the same amount; re-mark.

If you have made a shoulder adjustment, each back shoulder dart, if any, should be moved to the center of the new shoulder line and point to the shoulder blade. Adjust the spacing and length of any pleats or tucks in the bodice as needed.

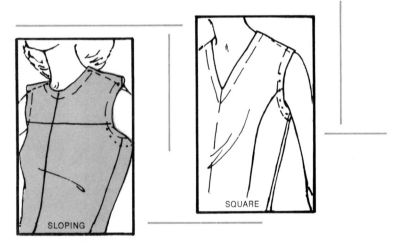

SLOPING

SQUARE

THE NECKLINE

The style referred to as the jewel neckline is the point from which all other necklines evolve. A styled neckline will vary from this basic neck-hugging fit according to how much higher or lower it is from the base of the neck.

You may have to raise or lower your neckline for a comfortable fit. An unclipped neckline may be misleading: Since the seamline is actually 5/8" (15mm) lower than the cut edge all around, the unclipped neckline will feel tighter than the finished neckline.

To lower a neckline, you may have to staystitch and clip before you decide to alter it. If you still feel the neckline is too tight or too high, take a marking pencil and mark a new seamline below the original wherever necessary. Perhaps you will need to lower it only in the front or back for a comfortable fit; if so, taper the new seamline to the original at the shoulder seam. Make small alterations and check the fit carefully before you proceed. Small amounts make a big difference on neckline seams, and once you have clipped, it is impossible to raise the neckline again.

The new seamline will have a larger circumference than the original, so you must also adjust any facings and collars that are stitched to the neckline. Measure the seamline of the original and adjusted neckline to determine how much longer the adjustment has made the length of the neckline seam. Lengthen the collar or facing along the center back seam an equal amount.

Facings and flat collars must be adjusted at the neckline seam identically to the bodice. Add an amount equal to the adjustment along the neckline edge of the collar or facing.

To raise a neckline, mark the new seamline above the original by the amount needed on the bodice front and/or back. If the neckline needs to be raised only in the front or back, taper the adjusted line to the original seamline at the shoulder seams.

This alteration must be done before you clip the neckline, so fit carefully. You will have a narrower than normal seam allowance, so staystitch along the new seamline to keep the neck seam stable.

You must also adjust any collars or facings. The new seamline will have a smaller circumference than the original; measure the seamline of both the original and adjusted neckline to determine the difference. Remove an equal amount at the center back of the collar and facing pattern pieces.

Facings and flat collars must be adjusted at the neckline identically to the bodice. Remove an amount equal to the adjustment from the neckline edge of the facing or collar as well.

Low necklines like V- or U-shapes may gape in your fashion fabric. Adjust by lifting the bodice front at the shoulder near the neck to remove excess fabric between bust apex and shoulder. Taper the adjustment to the armhole so the shoulder lies flat.

Test the fit of a low-cut neckline in muslin before cutting your fashion fabric. If, after you have cut your fashion garment, the neckline is still too low, try to pick up a bit of fabric in the shoulder seams as suggested for gaping necklines, or use a narrow neck seam allowance.

When fitting the neckline of a knit garment, handle your fabric gently. Some knits are very stretchy and should not be overhandled, pulled, or strained. Staystitch before fitting the neckline.

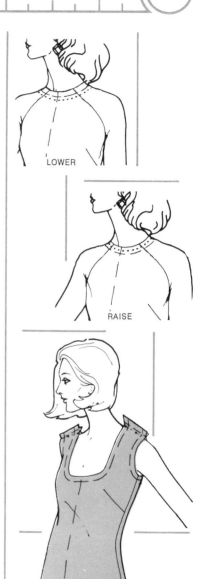

LOWER

RAISE

THE BACK AREA

Your garment should fit smoothly and be wrinkle-free across the back. If you find when fitting your fashion garment that there are horizontal or vertical wrinkles in the back, these can be corrected by changing the length or circumference of the bodice back, by re-marking seamlines, or by adjusting darts.

You may find that the center back seam of your garment is in need of some small adjustment. If a soft, stretchy fabric will not drape smoothly across the back and causes wrinkles, take in the center back seam a minimal amount. If your fabric is crisp and medium to heavy in weight, let out the center back seam a minimal amount for more ease. For a narrow back, see page 94. Note: When you adjust the back, the grain may chevron rather than balance; this is quite acceptable, but may be pronounced in stripes or plaids.

If the bodice back wrinkles above the shoulder blades, it may be due to a very erect back. When fitting, pin out excess fabric at the neck and shoulder, and reshape the darts to fit. The back neck and shoulder seam allowances will become larger, tapering to the original width at the armhole. If you have a rounded back,

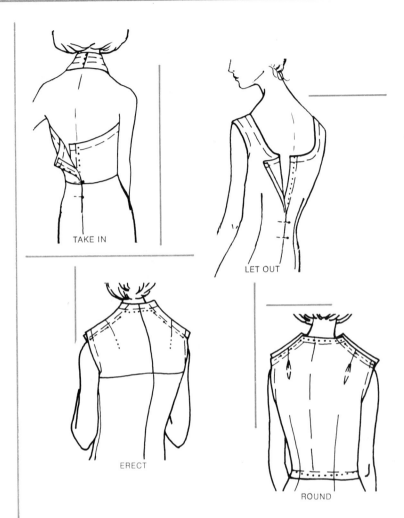

TAKE IN

LET OUT

ERECT

ROUND

the bodice back will pull up at shoulders and waist. When fitting, let out back shoulder and neck edges (seam allowances will become narrower), tapering to the original widgh at the

armhole. Reshape the darts to fit. For additional length, let out the waist seam across the center of the back, tapering to the original width at the sides.

128

THE BUST AREA

When fitting your fashion fabric in the bust area, you may be dealing with darts and geometric or contour seaming. Or no darts at all. It is the draping of these styled areas over your body contours that determines any minor fitting changes to be made in your fashion fabric. The weight and drape of your fabric and their effect on the wearing ease will influence minor changes in bust fit.

Fabric weight and drape affect the fit of darts built into your garment to accommodate body contours. The placement and depth of the darts control how the fabric will flow around your curves. Before changing a bust dart, adjust bra straps to the position that is most attractive and comfortable. Bust darts should end ½" to 1" (13mm to 25mm) from the apex of the bust. When repinning or rebasting each dart, be certain that it lies smoothly and unpuckered, and tapers to a point; see pages 81–90 for methods to make fitting changes. In medium- to heavy weight fabrics, a small dart will not lie flat; in this stage of fitting, do not be concerned.

Depending on fabric weight, you may need to change the

length or depth of the dart, or shift it slightly to avoid distorting the fabric design. Try to balance darts on the right and left sides of your garment even when your figure is asymmetrical.

To shorten or lengthen bust darts, determine the apex of the bust and mark with a pin. Draw new stitching lines with a marking pencil on the wrong side of the fabric. Begin with the original seamlines at the wide end and stitch, tapering to a new point ½" to 1" (13mm to 25mm) away from the apex. The change will affect how the wide end of the dart falls in the seam allowance. Press carefully and pin the dart at the seam allowances before you attempt to stitch across the dart. Failure to do this will result in puckering and/or pulling along the dart.

The underarm and front bust darts may need small changes if you find wrinkling and fullness across the bust. To decrease cupping, make darts

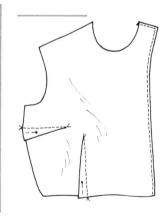

narrower, tapering toward the apex in a smooth point; take out an additional amount at the side and waist seam allowances of the bodice front. You may have to reshape the armhole seamline. Your garment may pull over the bust, and the waist may pull at the sides. To increase cupping, make darts deeper, tapering toward the apex in a smooth point. Let out side and waist seam allowances, and open your sleeve seams at the armhole the same amount.

Darts in knits may require a little more consideration. Because knitted fabrics have a tendency to cling, care must be taken to reduce the bulk of fabric layers and any ridges caused by undergarments. When darts are made in knits, they cling even closer to the body. When fitting darts in knit fabric, place pins close together, as knits are stretchy and the pins might fall out. Basting darts may be more appropriate.

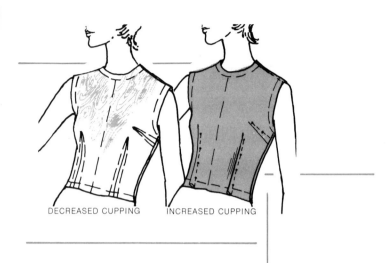

DECREASED CUPPING   INCREASED CUPPING

Eliminating a bust dart

Knit and bias-cut garments are naturals for fitting without darts, but other fabrics can also be fitted without darts. Remove basting from bust darts and underarm seams. Add an ease thread in dart area along underarm seam edge. Fit garment over bust, working out any excess fabric in armhole. Re-mark armhole seamline.

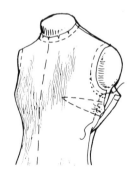

Geometric seaming

There are many geometric seaming details that incorporate bust
fit. When fitting garments of this type, do not fit too tightly over
body contours, as this distorts the fabric. The difficulty in fitting
garments with curved or angular seaming is in adjusting the
shaped seaming without destroying the balance and proportion.
In garments whose design is dependent on the proportion and
balance of decorative seaming, any change in seams to adjust the
fit may distort the fashion impact. Make small fitting changes in
the shoulder or side seams where they will be least obvious; keep
other seam changes to a minimum.

Princess seaming

The bust area should fit
smoothly over the apex of the
bust. If you find the fullest part
of the bustline shaping too
high or too low due to the
drape of your fashion fabric,
reshape the bustline seaming,
tapering smoothly to the original seamlines. For a princess
line that is too tight, release
and let out the seams over the
bust, tapering to the original
seamline above and below. For
a princess line that is too loose,
take in the seam allowances
over the bust area, retaining
the style line.

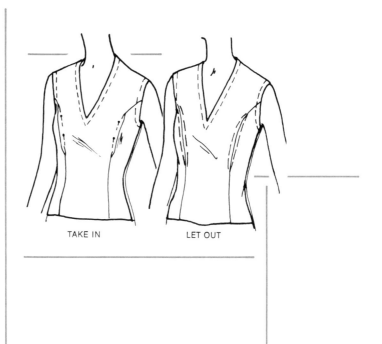

TAKE IN   LET OUT

THE ARMHOLE AREA

An evaluation of armhole and sleeve fit in your fashion fabric is essential as you proceed with your garment. This area is vital to comfortable fit, so approach each garment realistically—a jacket sleeve should not fit like a dress sleeve, nor a loose tunic top like a closely shaped fashion. Fit a jacket or coat over the garment you intend wearing under it, as the circumference must be large enough to accommodate the other garment.

A garment can be sleeveless or it may have sleeves—either set-in or raglan, which are made separately and attached to the garment, or kimono sleeves, which are extensions of the main bodice. Obviously there are many variations of these styles, and the fit of each is dependent upon the design. Your main concern is to obtain a comfortable and flattering garment, so approach your sleeve fit with that in mind.

Raglan

A raglan sleeve is joined to the garment with one continuous seam that runs diagonally from the front neckline to the underarm to the back neckline. As with the set-in sleeve, the design can vary; consider your specific pattern before you make any alterations.

Baste the shoulder darts or seams and underarm seams; then baste both sleeves into the garment. Test the sleeves with the arm relaxed and in motion. The sharpest curve of the shoulder dart or seam should fall over the shoulder hinge. Reshape the dart or seam to fit this contour, using the standard shoulder seam fitting adjustments (pages 63–67) as a guide. The underarm seam should fall about 1" (25mm) below the armpit, and arm movement should be free without pulling or straining. Remove basting across the underarm between the notches and raise or lower the underarm curve as needed, taking a deeper or narrower seam allowance on the bodice while maintaining the sleeve seam allowance; fit back and neck at the seam so the garment lies smoothly over these areas. Remember that the fit of raglan sleeves at the neck edge must be considered as well.

RAISE

LOWER

Kimono

The kimono sleeve is one of the easiest types to construct since it is merely an extension of the bodice. Often the sleeve is cut with a deep armhole, creating a soft drape of fabric under the arm with little or no fitting involved. If, however, it is cut to conform more to the curved shape around the shoulder with a shallower armhole opening, the fit becomes closer to the body and more attention to it is required.

The sharpest curve of the shoulder seam should fall over the shoulder; reshape the shoulder seam to fit if necessary.

The underarm seam must be reinforced before you baste since it will be necessary to clip to evaluate the fit; do so with discretion, since you can't unclip the seam allowance.

A close-fitting kimono sleeve usually involves a gusset—a small triangular or diamond-shaped piece of fabric that is inserted into the underarm seam for comfort and ease of movement. Your pattern guidesheet will give you specific instructions for applying the gusset.

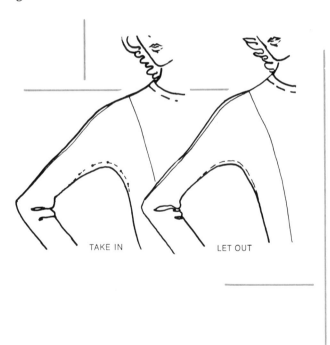

TAKE IN   LET OUT

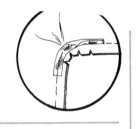

Set-in

As the name implies, these sleeves are set into the armhole of the garment. Variations are numerous: the cap can be softly rounded or gathered, the length long or short, the bottom shaped with darts, flared, or gathered. Refer to your pattern to determine the intended design.

On most standard set-in sleeves the sleeve should join the bodice just over the shoulder bone and fall smoothly without pulls or strain around the armhole. Its cap should cup smoothly, the arm portion should not wrinkle below the cupping, and the underarm seam should fall about 1″ (25mm) below the armpit. Since all your personal adjustments were built into the pattern pieces before you cut out your fashion fabric, the main concern now is adapting the sleeve as your fabric dictates.

Baste any elbow darts or adjust ease as you baste each sleeve seam. Ease threads can be added to the sleeve cap by hand or machine, depending on your fabric. Turn up the hem along the proposed hemline and pin, or apply any sleeve finish that will affect the sleeve length.

Pin the sleeve section to the armhole and adjust the ease; fasten the ease thread ends securely and then baste the sleeve in position for a fitting. Do not shrink the sleeve cap at this time. If you want to review the basics of setting in a sleeve, refer to *Vogue Sewing*.

To fit the sleeves, first check comfort and grain, then check sleeve fit from armhole to hem. If a loosely woven or knitted fabric is a trifle big, take in the sleeve a bit; in a bulky fashion fabric, you may let out the sleeve a bit if it is too snug. Taper any changes to the original armhole seamline. In a long sleeve without an opening, be sure that you have allowed enough room for your hand to slip through easily.

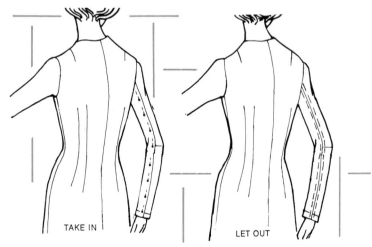

TAKE IN

LET OUT

Check sleeve cap, shoulder, and underarm areas. If the distribution of ease in the sleeve cap is not correct, see page 73. You must eliminate some excess ease from fabrics that will not smooth out to your satisfaction; these include certain synthetics treated for easy care. Fit the sleeve cap as explained on page 74. Remove the sleeve, then recut the cap area, using your altered pattern. Reset the sleeve into the garment to test the change in ease.

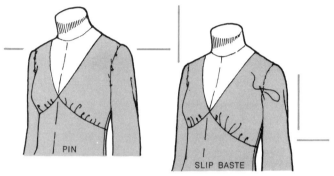

When working with bulky, heavy, stiff, tightly woven, or textured fabrics, the sleeve cap sometimes requires special handling. Unpin the sleeve cap after the ease threads have been fastened securely. Turn in the seam allowance along the ease threads and shape the sleeve cap smoothly; pin the sleeve cap in place as you work. Slip-baste the sleeve cap into position and test for proper fit and appearance before stitching permanently. Check the shoulder length and upper part of the armhole. Raise or lower the sleeve cap until the sleeve cap seamline is positioned on the bodice shoulder over the arm hinge. Rather than change the sleeve seam allowance, take a deeper or narrower seam allowance at the bodice shoulder.

If the underarm pulls or strains, make the seam adjustment that is made for raglan sleeves.

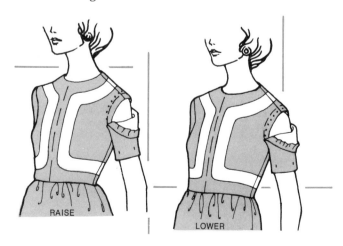

Sleeveless

The armholes on most sleeveless garments are cut to encircle the arm with the top seamline resting at the shoulder point. Refer to the fashion sketch and description of your pattern to determine if the design is a variation of this type. Many will have an extended shoulder line that drops over the shoulder, or a narrow shoulder width creating a halter-type design.

Regardless of the design, most sleeveless armholes should fall about 1" (25mm) below the armpit. If too tight, let out the shoulder and underarm seams, tapering to the original width; if too loose, take in the shoulder and underarm seams, tapering to the original width. Reshape the underarm area of the armhole if needed. Make the same changes on all facing seamlines.

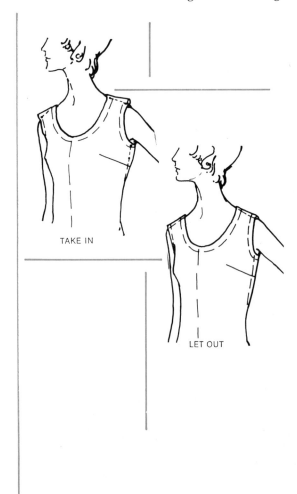

TAKE IN

LET OUT

THE WAIST AREA

The fit of the waist area is related closely to the fit of the midriff and hip area, as it is the starting point from which both are created.

Since you carefully built into the pattern pieces any necessary circumference adjustments, checking the waist fit at this point will not be difficult. The character of your fashion fabric may require a minor change—soft or stretchy fabrics may need to be taken in, while crisp or firm fabrics may need to be let out. Remember, the bulk of a pleated or gathered skirt will use up wearing ease when joined to a bodice—be careful not to overfit.

Waist

To take in the waist, divide the amount of change by the number of darts and/or seams; adjust each, tapering smoothly. To let out the waist, divide the amount of change by the number of darts and/or seams; adjust each, tapering smoothly.

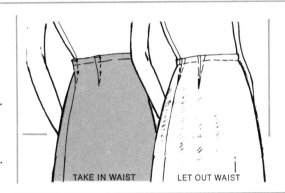

TAKE IN WAIST   LET OUT WAIST

Waist and midriff

To take in the waist, simply adjust the seams, taking in the side or other seams to fit the midriff and waist. Or, divide the amount of change by the number of darts and/or seams; adjust each, tapering smoothly and making sure you do not create too much cupping over the bust and back.

To let out, simply let out the side or other seams to fit the midriff and waist or other seams to fit the midriff and waist of your garment. Or, divide the amount of change by the number of darts and/or seams and then adjust each, tapering smoothly.

In a cut-in-one bodice and skirt, the shaping must be close

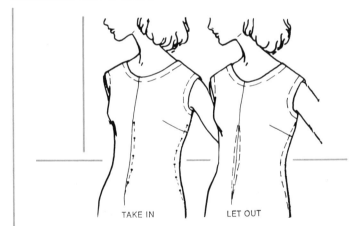

TAKE IN   LET OUT

to your needs, as you cannot now change it much. Fit the bodice from the waist working up; then fit the skirt from the waist to the hips working down.

If you are making a jacket or coat, repeat any changes in the lining.

Darts in skirts or skirt portions of a cut-in-one bodice and skirt are significant in that the waist and hips are crucial fitting areas. Special figure contours will affect the depth and placement of the darts (see pages 97–103). Baste these darts securely, since they will be subjected to much stress during fitting.

Waist seam

The seam that is the easiest one to evaluate on your garment is the one that falls at your waist. A raised or lowered waist seam should fall on the body as the designer originally planned, and should be fitted along with the midriff or hip area of your garment. Waist seams also give you an opportunity to adjust the hang of the skirt and to slightly adapt the bodice length. To adjust the bodice length to your needs, simply raise or lower the garment's waist seamline.

To improve the hang of your skirt, it may be necessary to raise or lower the waist in the front or back, or along its entire circumference.

Either procedure may require slight reshaping or respacing of darts. Cut-in-one bodice and skirts cannot be changed in length at the waist for a more evenly hanging skirt or pants.

Knits or other stretchy or loosely woven fabrics may need to be reinforced with tape to prevent stretching at the waist seam (see next page).

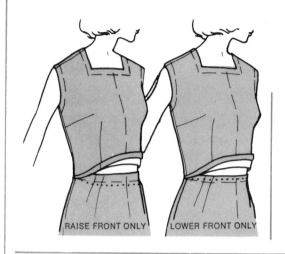

138

Swayback

Even though your pattern was altered, this problem may still be evident in soft fabrics: the skirt wrinkles across the back just below the waist. To fit, lift the skirt back, making seam allowances wider at the center back and tapering into the original width at the sides.
Reshape any darts to fit your body contour. This fitting change cannot be made after a cut-in-one bodice and skirt has been cut out.

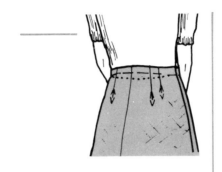

Applying a waistline stay

Waistline seams can be stayed to prevent stretching and to maintain a comfortable fit throughout the life of the garment. A stay will prevent the garment from riding up at the waistline and will relieve stress on the closure in that area as well.

A stay should be made of ½" to 1" (13mm to 25mm) wide, firmly woven tape or ribbon, such as grosgrain ribbon or cotton twill tape.

Cut the ribbon the exact length of the waistline seam plus 2" (5cm). Fold back each end ½" (13mm) and again ½" (13mm) and hand sew in place. Sew hooks and eyes to the ends, positioned so the ribbon meets without overlapping.

Pin the ribbon to the seam allowance on the skirt side with one edge along the waist seamline. Hand-tack the stay securely at side seams, darts, opening edges, etc., leaving at least 2" (5cm) free at each side of the opening so it can be fastened easily before the garment is closed.

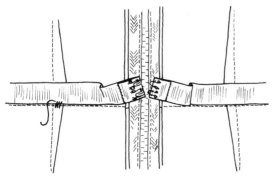

THE HIP AREA

A flattering fit through the hip area is essential for a professional look. Since it is fairly easy to determine any necessary adjustments in this area with measurements, it is most unlikely that you will need many alterations at this stage. However, certain figure characteristics or special fabrics may require additional refining.

Soft or stretchy fabrics may need to be taken in, and crisp or heavy fabrics may need to be let out. Any alterations made on the circumference of the garment can be done at the seamlines or by lowering or raising the waistline, depending on the type of correction needed. Any minor uneven figure characteristics, such as one high hip, can often be handled more easily at this point on the fabric rather than by cutting two separate pattern pieces.

To take in the hip area, pin the skirt along the seamline to fit, and mark the new seamline with a marking pencil. Stitch, and trim away the excess seam allowance.

To let out in the hip area, release the seams, pin to fit, mark the new seamlines with a marking pencil, and stitch. If you don't have enough excess seam allowance to make the alteration, you can raise the skirt slightly all around and mark a new waistline seam. Position the skirt for a comfortable hip fit, tie a string around your waist to determine your natural waistline and mark the new waist seamline with a marking pencil. Adjust the waistline circumference as necessary. This technique may require lengthening any darts as well. Also, it will not work for straight, slim skirts.

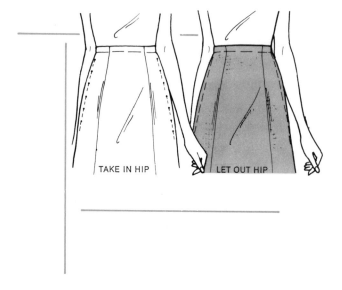

TAKE IN HIP   LET OUT HIP

Protruding hip bones

Usually noticed only in fitted garments, this characteristic causes the fabric to pull across the front. Crisp and heavy fabrics may accent the problem. To fit, reposition and reshape darts over hip bones; if a larger circumference is needed, let out the front at the side seams. A cut-in-one bodice and skirt that has been cut out cannot be fitted as well as a waist-seamed garment. Reposition and reshape darts, letting out seams slightly.

One high hip

In a fitted garment this characteristic pulls the skirt off grain. You may need to use a narrower waist seam allowance on the high hip side and a wider one on the other side to align the grain. Adjust dart length if necessary. This change cannot be made in a cut-in-one bodice and skirt after it has been cut out.

Flat buttocks

The skirt collapses for want of body support, a condition more visible in soft fabrics. To fit, make darts shallower; smooth excess fabric toward the side seams, making the back side seam allowances wider and retaining the waist fit across the back. For a cut-in-one bodice and skirt, make darts shallower in the skirt area and work out excess fabric at the sides or back seams. Take in the center back seam slightly, if you find that further correction is needed.

Large buttocks

Firm and heavy fabrics may emphasize this figure characteristic. The skirt back rides up and pulls the side seams. To fit, lower the skirt back, making the seam allowance narrower across the center back and tapering to the original width at the sides. Let out the back at the seams for greater circumference. Shorten and re-shape darts to fit. Only minimal fitting can be done in a cut-in-one bodice and skirt that has been cut out; darts and seams can be let out and darts reshaped.

Large abdomen

Crisp and heavy fabrics may emphasize this figure characteristic. The front rides up and pulls the side seams. To fit, lower the front, making the seam allowance narrower across the center front and tapering to the original width at the side seams. Let out the front at the side seams if greater circumference is needed; shorten and reshape darts to fit. Only minimal fitting can be done at front darts and side seams in a cut-in-one bodice and skirt that has been cut out.

141

Design Features

At this point you should have made all the alterations necessary to refine the fit of the garment. Double-check to make certain that all the changes are accurate and that the garment fits to perfection. Refer to page 121 to review once again the fitting checklist before you proceed.

A list of any refinement changes you have made can be helpful as you approach the addition of design features. It will provide an instant reminder to check for any necessary alterations on corresponding pieces. For instance, if you made a neckline alteration you will also have to alter the collar; if you made a waistline change you may have to change the waistband.

Any pattern tissue adjustments that you made before you cut your fabric should have already been made on the corresponding pattern pieces. Keep this in mind as you proceed to refine the design of your fashion garment.

GATHERS, VENTS, TUCKS, AND PLEATS

Carefully controlled fullness is the rationale behind designers' use of pleats, gathers, tucks, and vents. Aesthetically, these design features add visual interest and dimension; practically, they allow extra room for mobility and comfort. Any woman can wear each of these four design elements successfully if she has first analyzed her figure to gain an understanding of how much controlled fullness is flattering to her, and where to use it to best advantage.

Pleats are folds of fabric which may be sharply pressed or softly rolled with no pressing; they may be edgestitched along the fold for a defined silhouette or they may be left to fall freely with no stitching. Tucks can be stitched on either the inside or the outside of the garment; they can be a decorative as well as a functional design feature and may be released at one or both ends to add design fullness. Gathers are the simplest means by which controlled fullness can be incorporated in a design. They can be skimpy and hang straight or they can be full, billowy, and stand away from the body. Vents are two fabric layers with an opening; they allow for action and then return to their original position, where they are usually inconspicuous. Whatever form controlled fullness takes in your garment, there is an easy way to adapt the fabric to your needs. Success with these design features begins with accurate marking and basting to make fitting easier.

Gathers

Your fabric choice will play an important role in the performance of gathers. Crisp or lightweight fabrics may billow too much over the hips, while stiff or heavyweight fabric may cup and fall into awkward folds. How the fabric reacts to the gathers and your figure must be discerned at this point. If needed, you can fit out some of the excess at each seam or you can dart it out at the waist. Darting it out will not affect the sweep of the skirt, and is the best technique when the gathers form excessive bulk at the waist seam. Space long darts evenly throughout the

skirt at the waist. When the desired effect has been achieved, stitch the darts permanently; trim to ⅝″ (15mm), and press open, then form the gathers. For stiff or heavy fabrics, it may be necessary to reduce the skirt sweep to maintain the silhouette. Fit out excess at each seam for desired effect.

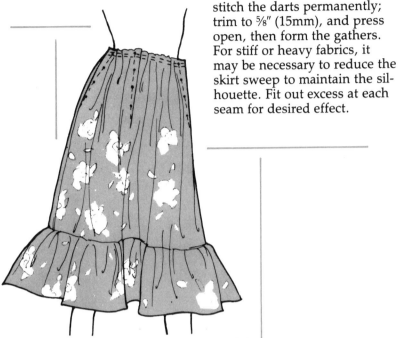

Vents

This is an opening formed by an overlapped edge and an underlapped edge; it is found at the end of a seam. A vent will require fitting if it spreads or twists. Be sure the upper ends of the vent are supported properly before you begin. If the circumference needs to be adjusted through the vent area of the garment, the vent edges will becoome correspondingly deeper or narrower. Taper any changes above the vent gradually to the garment seamline; the garment above the vent must be smooth for the vent to lie flat.

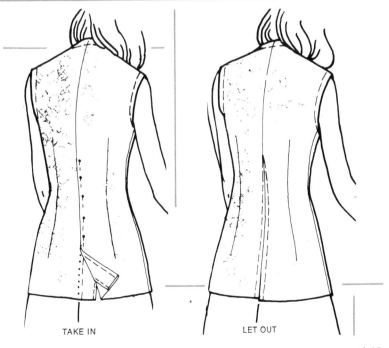

TAKE IN   LET OUT

143

Tucks

These may need fitting attention, especially if they are over body contours or are controlling the circumference. Simply divide the amount of change needed by the number of tucks and increase or decrease tuck width accordingly, or increase or decrease the number of tucks.

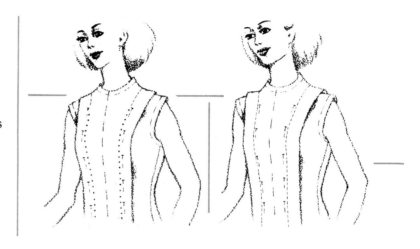

Pleats

Single pleats or clusters of pleats used as a focal point do not present problems, as these are never fitted—the fitting is done in the other vertical seams. However, should a single pleat include an underlay and incorporate the closure, simply increase or decrease the circumference by taking in or letting out at the foldline or roll line. Use a wider or narrower seam allowance on the pleat extension.

Careful planning is needed for all-around pleats, as might be found in a skirt. Complete the hem before basting the pleats in place. Then form the pleats from the hem up. This takes the guesswork out of fitting; any unwanted length can be worked out at the waist or other seam in which they will be joined. Circumference adjustment will be required if pleats sag and overlap, or if they twist and pull.

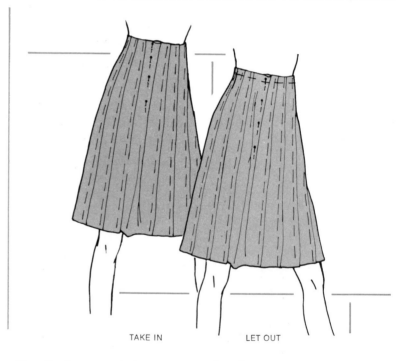

TAKE IN   LET OUT

To adjust garment circumference at this time, release only one pleat to see the extent of the change needed; take in or let out that one pleat until the skirt fits correctly. Remove the skirt and divide the amount of change equally among all of the pleats. The secret of fitting straight pleats is to retain the original foldlines or roll lines by making any changes along the indicated placement lines.

Pleats can also be fitted for

144

waist and hip circumference. Fit the waist, tapering to the hip; or fit the hip, tapering to waist; you can also fit to accommodate both circumferences. Naturally, the pleats will become deeper or narrower when the hip area requires fitting. Shaped pleats whose upper portion has been cut away to reduce bulk can be fitted similarly.

In order for pleats to hang properly, grainline must be maintained below the hipline. It is often impossible to keep the grain perfect above the hipline because of the shaping involved.

If the fabric you are using has a definite vertical design such as a plaid or stripe, position any alterations to conform to the design.

Pleats should hang straight without spreading or overlapping. If pleats overlap at the hemline, lower the waistline seam until they hang correctly. If pleats spread open at the hemline, raise the waistline seam until the pleats hang correctly. You may find this alteration necessary in only one section of the waistline, since the problem could be a result of one high hip, a sway back, a large abdomen, etc.

When your garment's pleats have been fitted to your satisfaction, machine baste along the waist seamline to secure

the folds, seam allowances, and/or the underlaps. Pleats that are to be permanently creased should be pressed at this time. Soft pleats should be steam-pressed, pinned, and smoothed gently by hand to drape nicely. Remove all basting except at the waist seamline and then try on your garment again.

After your pleats have been made final and everything has been stitched permanently, you may find that they still require some refinement. If you feel that the pleats need edgestitch-

ing to hold a sharp crease, do this before joining them to the garment or waistband and after completing the hem. If your fashion fabric needs some additional help to support the weight of the pleats, shape a stay of underlining or other lightweight, durable fabric.

COLLARS

Careful fitting can create a collar that is a fashion highlight and an expression of the best of your sewing abilities. It is important that you maintain the same fitting standards—whether your collar is a shape variation of the flat, rolled, or standing collar, or is a combination of two, like a notched or shawl collar.

If collar construction and shaping have been one of your problems, review the instructions in *Vogue Sewing*. You must build the right amount of fabric into the collar so the upper collar will roll smoothly over the undercollar. This will result in a finished collar that lies softly on the garment without curling; the seam will be invisible along the outer edges, and the collar will rise gently from the garment neckline.

Your garment shell plays a most important part in a successfully fitted collar. Be sure to check any changes you have made in the shoulder and neck areas. If you raised or lowered the neckline, or adjusted the shoulder or back, the neck seamline circumference may be larger or smaller than that of the collar. Measure along the marked neck seamlines on the garment and the original neck seamline on the collar. Should there be any discrepancy, correct the collar as follows:

For fitting changes of less than 1" (25cm), ease the collar slightly to the garment, or ease the garment slightly to the collar; this should not affect the rise and roll of the collar. Baste and test (see below); since the change recommended is less than ¼" (6mm) on each quarter of the neck seamline, it should result in a well-fitted collar. However, if your fabric is stiff, crisp, or bulky, and does not ease well as you shrink out the fullness, the depth of the seam allowance may be adjusted on the collar until it fits properly.

For fitting changes of 1" (25mm) or more, cut the collar in muslin and test-fit before cutting your fashion fabric. Increase or decrease the length of muslin collar so all position markings match at centers and shoulders. Transfer the changes to the pattern, then cut and construct the fashion fabric collar, testing as explained below.

Many collars are prepared, then sandwiched between the garment and the facing. Others have an undercollar stitched to the garment, an upper collar stitched to the facing, and are then joined to the garment's outer edges. A third type of collar finishes the garment edge without a facing.

To fit a finished collar, lap the collar neck edge over the garment, matching seamlines, centers, and shoulders. Try on the garment or put it on your dress form to fit. Use the pattern envelope illustrations as a guide to check the appearance of the collar. The collar should lie symmetrically against both halves of the garment at the closing and where a two-section collar meets.

146

A rolled collar can hug the neck or stand away from it, but the fit is the same. The roll should smoothly and evenly encircle the neck; it should not ride high or low, and the finished edge of the collar should cover the back neck seamline. Fit to your satisfaction; mark the established roll line and any changes.

A flat collar is one of the basic collar styles from which all others are derived. It may require clipping at even intervals to appear as it should. Mark any changes on the neckline and then remove the collar from the garment.

A standing collar can be crisp and military, or it can be a molded bias one that turns down over itself. The crisp standing collar is applied to the garment and adjusted until it fits correctly; clip seam allowances if necessary; remember that the inner layer is usually used to finish the neck seam. Mark changes in seamlines before removing.

The finished edge of the bias standing collar should be turned down so that it just covers the neck seamline. Stretch the collar gently to mold smoothly. Baste along the established roll through all thicknesses; mark seamline changes before removing the collar.

A collar whose undercollar is sewn to the garment and whose upper collar is sewn to the facing is handled as follows: lap and baste the undercollar to the garment. Begin the roll for the collar and/or lapels as indicated in the pattern illustration for your

147

design. Roll the collar smoothly and make sure the collar seamline will fall just below the back neck seamline. Mark the roll and any seamline changes; remove the collar. Stitch the undercollar to the garment permanently. Then baste the facing unit together, lapping and basting the upper collar to its neck edge if there is a separate section. Place collar and facing unit over the garment, matching neck seamlines; baste. With your garment wrong side out, fit the collar and facing to the garment, shaping carefully along the established roll. Mark any changes in the seamline of the upper collar and facing before removing.

A notched or convertible collar begins to shape from the top buttonhole marking. Adjust at the neck seamlines if needed. The finished collar edge should cover the back neck seamline. To check the closed position when the collar ends meet, turn in the corner of the overlap as illustrated. The ends will then lie smoothly and you can test the fit. When satisfied with the fit, mark the roll on both collar and lapels. Then turn to page 150 for information on fitting the closure. Always allow for the roll of the lapels when you fit either the applied or the extended type of facing.

The secret of a beautifully draped cowl is to make a stay cut on the straight grain, using your permanent pattern as a guide. Cut the stay from the lining fabric; then construct, finishing the neck edge with a narrow binding. Baste the stay to the cowl along the outer edges, easing the cowl to fit; avoid stretching. Baste the cowl in place and lap its edge over the garment; match seamlines.

Mold and shape your cowl on a dress form, basting back edges together as they fall. It is recommended that you use weights if necessary to control the drape of the cowl.

UNDERCOLLAR

UPPER COLLAR/FACING

148

INSET BANDS

Inset bands can be an important design feature of a garment, such as the finishing edge of a neckline, armhole, sleeves, or hem, or they can be a functional feature, such as a center front placket. They can take many shapes and must be considered seriously when fitting your fashion garment.

To prepare the garment for fitting, baste any of these pieces to the corresponding garment section. In some instances they become part of the main pattern pieces, and it is impossible to proceed with the garment until these pieces have been joined and fitted with the main garment pieces.

Maintain a uniform finished width for the entire length of a band at neck and armhole edges. Should you make any fitting changes in these areas, adjust band seamlines accordingly.

Inset bands at the waist are basted to the bodice and skirt. When fitting, allow for later fabric bulk; do not overfit. For soft fabrics, underline an inset section that must support a full skirt.

Bands used as a hem finish influence the length and drape of your fabric, so consider the total garment length before cutting the fabric. If your hem band is doubled, join its ends and fold it wrong sides together. Lap and baste band to garment; raise, lower, increase, or decrease as needed.

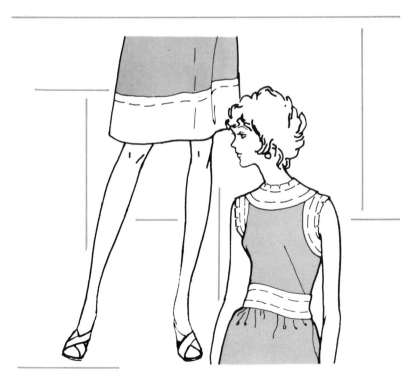

CLOSURES

Before making a closure permanent, it requires close evaluation. Not only must a closure be smooth and flat, but the items—zippers, buttons, snaps, decorative closures—must work with your fashion fabric without overwhelming the garment or pulling the closure out of line. If your closure includes a facing, it must be fitted at the same time.

Match the center front or center back markings on overlapped edges (A). Pin in place and reposition buttonhole or other closure markings so they fall at the bust, waist, and hip; this prevents the opening from gaping over your body contours.

You can substitute smaller buttons and increase their number, but your lap will not take larger buttons because the extension was designed for a specific button size. Evenly respace any markings that have been changed. Mark where a snap or hook is needed to support opening edges. To avoid distortion, consider the weight and flexibility of the closure.

Edges that meet should be basted in position to evaluate the fit before applying the closure (B). Mark the position of the closure, repositioning as necessary. As with lapped edges, it is extremely important to consider the weight and flexibility of the closure that will be used on these edges.

Garments with asymmetrical openings should be handled in a similar manner (C). Refer to your pattern to determine how the garment should be positioned. Edges that are designed off grain must be handled with care to avoid stretching. Stay the edges with stretched bias tape if necessary.

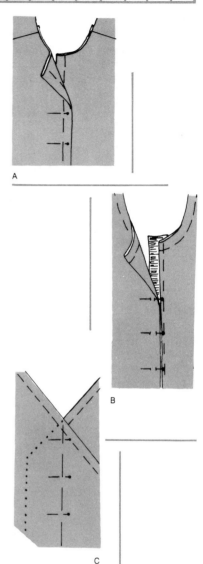

Buttons

When choosing your buttons consider their weight. A button too heavy for the fabric can distort the fit of the garment by causing gaping or pulling. Make certain the button is placed directly beneath the buttonhole or it will pull. Add a thread shank to a sew-through button to maintain a smooth fit. In heavy garments such as a coat, an additional thread shank may be necessary with shank buttons.

Reposition button and buttonhole markings as necessary.

Zippers

Baste the zipper to the garment by your chosen method of application and try on the garment. The closure must lie smoothly and be flat; its weight should not distort the fabric. Make sure the length is appropriate for your figure—replace the zipper with another length if it ends at an awkward area; move a side zipper to a center front or back seam in a skirt if your hip curves look asymmetrical.

   For stretchy or bias fabrics, stabilize opening edges with stretched bias tape (ribbon seam binding is usually too rigid for these edges).

   To insert a zipper in strechable knits, pin the opening edges to the zipper tape while the garment is in its stretched condition on your body. Remove the garment and baste securely for a test fit— the zipper area may wrinkle or twist when the fabric is relaxed, but it will fit perfectly when the garment is worn.

POCKETS

Now check to make certain that the finished pocket is perfect on the garment. The small details involved add up to a fashion garment of which you can be proud. Check the flap or welt and make sure that it is flat and smooth. If the edges of a flap turn up, they can be tacked securely in place about ½" (13mm) from the top; take care that the stitching does not show on the outside. The garment must have enough wearing ease in the pocket area to accommodate the pocket type—patch, those inserted in a slash, side slant, or in-seam. Pockets should curve smoothly over the body with the garment; there should be no pulls or puckers in the garment around the pocket.

   If you plan to add a decorative button or buckle, check to see that its weight can be supported by the pocket without distorting the shape or opening. At this time, a little spot pressing will make your pockets crisp and fresh; steam-press to shrink out any slightly stretched areas of the pocket opening.

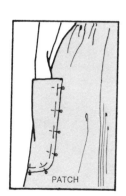

PATCH

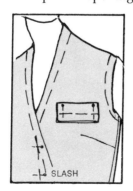

SLASH

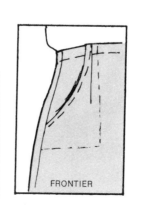

FRONTIER

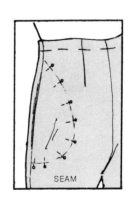

SEAM

151

Pocket placement

Functional pockets positioned below the waist should be placed where your hands can slip into them comfortably and should be deep enough for your hands. Pockets above the waist are usually decorative; place them where they will be most flattering and balanced. Curvaceous women should generally avoid flap or patch pockets. Eliminate a pocket or pare down its proportions to make the most of the design while still maintaining attractive dimensions.

Before placing pockets, any fitting changes in your garments should be resolved. Thread-trace the grainlines, so you will be able to align the grain of the pocket, welt, or flap with the grain of your garment. Turn in seam allowances of a patch pocket, welt, or flap; baste. A side slant pocket is part of the garment shell and must be basted in place for the first fitting. Baste the shaped edges of the pocket and the garment together, and baste side and waist edges together along the seamline before a fitting. A garment with inside pocket sections requires more wearing ease so the pockets will not leave a ridge or an outline on the garment. Pin patch pockets, flaps, or welts over placement markings, keeping grains aligned. Do not hesitate to shift them to a more flattering position.

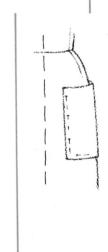

Pocket placement in knits depends on the character of the fabric with which you are working. Though there is great diversity in knits, some of the characteristic drape and performance is not predictable, and it is here that we must issue a word of caution about pockets: make sure you do not overfit, as pocket imprints will show through. In the stable knits, most pocket treatments are appropriate. In moderate stretch or stretch knits, where there must be give on the body, it is often best to avoid pockets. Patch pockets on stretchy knits are feasible only if you fit them carefully to the garment over your body contours.

Pockets should lie flat and smooth, and should not gape open. If a pocket is placed over a body contour, pin it in place carefully so that it is slightly curved over the body. Do not baste it taut, as this will distort the fit of the garment.

Garments having pockets that are set into seams need enough extra ease for the pocket and your hand. Their placement must be planned before the garment is cut out. In medium to heavyweight fabrics, do not overfit, as the pocket may gape open due to lack of wearing ease. These pockets should be invisible; the opening should lie flat and smooth.

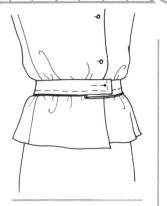

WAISTLINE FINISHES

Proper fit of your waistline finish is essential for the comfort and perfect drape of your fashion. Regardless of the finish you choose, care and attention will now be rewarded with a flattering and comfortable garment.

Waistbands

Any pattern tissue adjustments made at your waistline should have been made on your waistband as well. Any additional alterations made throughout the fitting should also be accounted for on the waistband.

With interfacing basted in place, fit the waistband. Fold a straight waistband in half lengthwise. Pin all fabric layers of a contour waistband together after basting the seams. First fit the waistband without the garment; place it on the body where it will fall when completed. Increase or decrease circumference as needed, allowing for bulk and being careful not to overfit. Then fit it with the garment as explained for a waist seam.

The width of the waistband can be altered if necessary. You may find the band too wide or too narrow for your body proportions. For a straight waistband simply determine the width that is comfortable and flattering, then re-mark the seamlines along the length of the waistband.

Width can be altered on contour waistbands as well, but the alteration will change the circumference measurement. Remove width from the top of the waistband and adjust the circumference accordingly.

TAKE IN

Elastic casings

To fit an elasticized-waist finish, put your garment on and pin the elastic around your waist. Pull up the extension and analyze the waist and hip area.

To fit, take in or let out as needed, making sure to leave enough room to put on and take off the garment easily. Mark your garment along the upper edge of the elastic and use this line for the foldline of the casing.

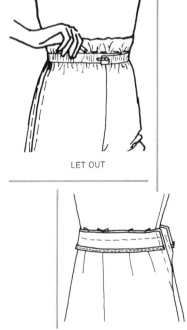

LET OUT

Facings

Some waistlines are finished with a facing, in which case the top of the garment should fall exactly on the waistline. Any pattern tissue adjustments made on the skirt should also have been made on the facings. Any additional alterations should be incorporated into the facing. It's helpful to stay the waistline with seam binding to prevent stretching and to maintain a perfect waistline fit throughout the life of the garment.

153

SLEEVE FINISHES

Many sleeve finishes will add length to your sleeve and must be in position when you are fitting. Cuffs—either turnback or extended—and applied bands are a part of the total sleeve length. Other sleeve finishes may be sandwiched between the sleeve edge and a facing; these do not affect the sleeve length, but may necessitate minor fitting at the hem.

If your sleeve has an opening that will be slashed, do not complete the opening until the sleeve has been fitted. For a sleeve with pleats or gathers, baste pleats in place and add the gathering threads so the sleeve can be adjusted to fit the finish.

Cuffs or bands

To prepare cuffs or bands for a fitting, include any underlining or interfacing. Fold a cuff or band with an extended facing wrong sides together, and baste ends and upper edges along the seamlines. For a two-section cuff or band, baste the layers along the lower edge and then turn along the basted seam. With wrong sides together, baste ends and upper edge. Lap the ends of the band or cuff, matching seamlines; baste.

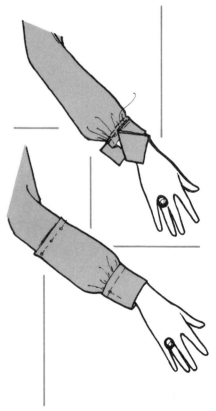

Lap the cuff or band over the sleeve, matching seamlines; baste. When ready to fit, match markings and use pins to fasten a cuff with a closure as it will be worn.

After basting the sleeve into the armhole (or applying the finish to or pinning up the hem of a raglan or kimono sleeve), check the fit and length of the sleeve.

Increase or decrease the circumference at the opening edges or at the ends that were lapped; adjust the sleeve circumference to fit the finish. Do not overfit—heavy or bulky fabrics will use up wearing ease when the cuff or band is completed; for a finish without an opening, allow enough room to slip your hand through. If the pleated or gathered area is too stiff or full, remove some fullness by eliminating a few gathers or decreasing the width of the pleats.

With the cuff or band in place, check the sleeve length and design fullness. Increase or decrease the sleeve length without changing the depth of the finish unless your fabric dictates—in stiff or heavy fabrics it may be necessary to take from the seam allowance of the finish too. If these fabrics do not assume the correct silhouette when gathered or pleated, adapt the circumference as previously suggested.

Mark any changes on both the sleeve and the cuff or band finish. Remove both the sleeve and the sleeve finish from a set-in sleeve; remove the sleeve finish from a kimono or raglan sleeve that is part of your garment shell.

Elastic casings

To fit an elasticized sleeve finish, put your garment on and pin the elastic around your wrist. Adjust the length of the elastic needed, making sure you leave enough length for it to slip over your hand easily as well as to accommodate the bulk of the fabric created by the casing. Mark the length needed and allow additional length for the overlap. Check the sleeve length and adjust along the lower edge of the sleeve if necessary.

Other sleeve finishes

Check the sleeve length. Adjust a short, elbow, three-quarter, bracelet, or full-length sleeve so the hem edge parallels the floor. Mark any changes made in hemlines or seamlines.

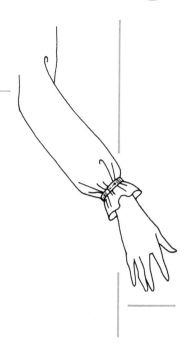

LININGS

Fitting the lining is an essential step in achieving a durable, attractive fashion. The garment should be free of wrinkles and distortion, and the lining should not cause bubbles or ridges on the surface of the fashion fabric. If your lining fabric is not compatible with your fashion fabric, a badly shaped garment will result. It may be wise to forgo cutting out the lining until you have fitted the garment. If you have made any changes when fitting your garment, repeat these on your lining before cutting. If you will be using a bulky lining or interlining, refer to page 157 before cutting either your fashion fabric or the lining.

  Coats and jackets are usually lined, and your pattern will include pieces for the lining. Dresses, skirts and pants do not usually require a lining. If you wish to line them for luxury, durability, or comfort and need construction advice, see the instructions in *Vogue Sewing.*

  Ideally your lining should be a fraction smaller in circumference than the fashion garment into which it will be inserted. However, a lining that is considerably smaller will be uncomfortable, and will wear due to strain. Conversely, a lining that is too big for the garment might affect the fit because its extra bulk uses up wearing ease.

  Regardless of garment style, fitting a lining is an easy feat in the completion of your garment. Baste the lining shell together, repeating in it any changes in fit made in the garment; leave the appropriate seam open for a zipper or other closure. Linings are always pinned into the garment so the wrong sides are together. All lining centers, seams, and darts should be matched to those of the garment. Put pleats, gathers, and ease threads in the lining if the addition of these are indicated by the design of your garment.

Skirts

Place the lining shell inside the garment. Pin, matching all centers, darts, and seams; if necessary, ease the garment to fit the lining at the upper edge. Turn in the opening edges to clear the zipper teeth. Baste the upper and opening edges together and try on the garment for a fitting. Make any changes until both layers mold together smoothly without any bubbling or pulling.

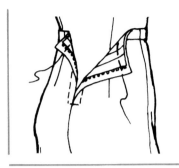

Coats and jackets

The linings discussed at this point are to be made from standard light- and medium-weight lining fabrics. When coats or jackets are interlined or when the lining fabric is bulky, the lining cannot be fitted successfully after the garment has been completed. Turn to page 157 for fitting directions.

When fitting a lining, you must compensate for the reaction of your lining to the fashion fabric. Baste the back pleat in place, and leave the shoulder seams open as you join the lining shell. Place the lining inside the garment, matching the back pleat to the center back marking or seam. Working toward the front edges, match seamlines and baste. Match armhole and neck seamlines; then lap shoulder edges. Again, match seamlines and baste. Try the garment on and test its fit. Shoulder pads may create excess fabric through the shoulder area of both front and back, so eliminate any wrinkles by working them out at the shoulder seam. When you see that the two layers are working as one, mark the changes and then remove the lining for construction. When the lining shell has been permanently inserted into the garment but the hem has not been sewn, you are ready to fit the sleeves.

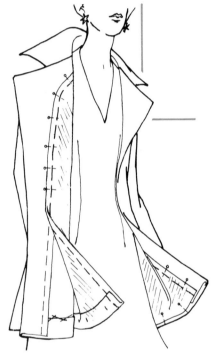

Fitting sleeve linings demands care; they should be slightly smaller in circumference than the garment sleeves to ensure a comfortable and smooth fit in your completed garment. Baste the sleeve seams, adding any darts or ease threads at the elbows. Add ease threads to the sleeve caps. Insert each sleeve lining in the appropriate garment sleeve. Lap the armhole edges, matching seamlines; pin, adjust ease, and baste. Shape each sleeve cap and sleeve lining inside the garment, adjusting as needed. Mark changes determined in the fitting and remove the sleeve linings.

After lining sleeves have been permanently inserted in the garment, turn to page 160 for directions on completing the lining hems of both the garment and the sleeves.

Underlining

Fitting a garment with underlining requires a keen eye. Look for imprints of bubbles or ridges in the underlining that interfere with the smoothness of your fashion fabric. If this occurs, release the seams, darts, or opening edges, and, working with the grain, eliminate the underlining problems. Underlining may also interfere with the hang of the garment if both grains have not been aligned correctly; wrinkles or pulling may appear along a seam. Correct this as you would any grain distortion.

Dresses

Dress linings are usually fitted immediately after the garment shell has been fitted, so edges can be finished with the facings, sleeves, and collars. Place the lining shell inside the garment; pin, matching all centers, darts, and seams. Ease the garment to fit the lining at neck and armhole edges, and turn in the opening edges to clear the zipper teeth or other closures. Baste neck, armhole, and opening edges together, and try on the garment for a fitting. Make changes as suggested on page 155 until both layers mold together. If the dress fabric irritates your skin, cut facings from the lining fabric as well. To line sleeves, refer to the information on page 156 for coats and jackets.

Bulky linings

Adding bulky linings to outerwear provides a luxurious finish along with added comfort and warmth. Bulky linings can be decorative as well as insulating and are often added to coats, suits, jackets, and vests. When one thinks of bulky linings, fur or furlike fabrics immediately come to mind, but there are other types as well, such as quilted satin. Even brushed cotton flannels teamed with denim produce unexpectedly warm sportswear jackets. Whatever fashion impression you wish to make, there is a bulky lining that will accomplish it.

Choose a bulky lining fabric that is compatible with your outer fabric. Care requirements should be the same and the outer fabric must be able to sustain the weight and bulk of the lining.

Cut wider seam allowances in both your lining and the outer fabric to allow for alterations. Unlike traditional linings where the garment is constructed and the lining is then fitted, a bulky lining is fitted first and then the outer garment is fitted over it. Place the right side of the bulky lining next to your body. If the garment is part of an ensemble, fit the bulky lining over the inner garment.

Make any necessary alterations on the lining, then pin the shoulders of the lining and outer fabric together and position the garment correctly on your body. Fit the outer garment so that it molds smoothly over the lining. Evaluate the fit and alter accordingly.

Sleeve linings can be cut from bulky lining fabrics but you may find it more flattering and comfortable to cut them from a coordinating light- to medium-weight lining fabric. If you are relying on the bulky lining fabric for warmth, you can underline the sleeves with flannel or lambswool.

FACINGS

The fit of a facing should be smooth and flat so that the faced area has little bulk. It should be reinforced with interfacing and may be taped to reduce the chances of stretching. In addition to a flat, smooth fit, you should strive for durability. Facings can be found at the neckline, armholes, waistline and sometimes at the hemlines of sleeves and skirts. Before fitting, make any changes in the facing that have been made in the garment. If you have raised or lowered the neckline, adjusted the shoulder seam and the underarm area or raised or lowered the waist seamline, transfer these changes to the facing.

Baste applied facings to the garment along the seamline. Fold extended facings back along the foldline and pin to secure to the garment.

Neckline edges may require clipping at even intervals in order for them to fit, while armhole edges may require that only the underarm curve be clipped. When fitting a waist facing on a skirt or on pants, ease the garment to the facing as indicated by your pattern. Strive for a smooth fit over the hips.

When fitting knitted or stretch fabrics, avoid overhandling. If you find, in heavy or bulky fabrics, that facings leave a ridge or imprint on the outside of your garment, replace the self-fabric with one of lightweight fabric.

If your fashion garment includes a collar or other features sandwiched between the garment and facing, this must be fitted before you attach the facing permanently. The same applies to a facing that finishes a closure edge. You must fit the collar, then the facing, as any change will affect all three garment areas.

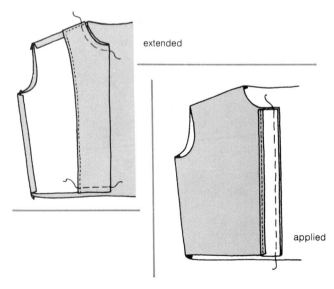

extended

applied

LAYERED FITTING

It is essential that you have a thorough understanding of wearing ease and style ease because the key to fitting layered garments lies in these concepts. Layering demands consideration when choosing your pattern before cutting into your fashion fabric and again when fitting. The relationship of each fabric layer and its reaction to the layer next to it is variable.

Garments presented in the Vogue Patterns catalogue as a total layered look have built-in wearing ease for each layer. Jacket and coat patterns have extra ease so they can be worn over other garments. However, a jacket that is a cut-off version of a coat cannot be worn under the coat, as the two have the same wearing ease. Likewise, separates chosen at random to make up a layered ensemble need special consideration, as they may not have been created to work as you plan to use them. Cut wider seam allowances to build a safety factor into your fabric. When fitting, start with the layer closest to the body and work outward. With each additional layer, the amount of ease will be slightly greater to accommodate the previous layers. If a bulky lining is added, refer to page 157 before you begin cutting out and fitting your fabric.

When fitting layered garments, be sure not to fit out the wearing ease, and be constantly aware of your fashion silhouette to avoid overfitting and loss of style lines. Layered fitting pertains not only to cold-weather ensembles, but also includes swimsuits with succeeding layers of cover-up fashions.

HEMS

Earlier in the process of fitting you pinned up a trial hem to judge the fit and proportions of your emerging garment. Now the time has come to perfect your hem. Before you start, there are several factors to consider—the proper undergarments, shoes or boots, and any fashion accessories that will affect the proportion of the design must be worn when determining the proper length for your newly created garment. If your fashion includes a belt, wear it when working on the hem, as your garment will be shortened when the belt is secured around your body.

For centuries, hem length was dictated by fashion. Today's best hem length is one that helps to create a total and successful fashion look. A hem length must perfect the proportion of the silhouette and the drape of the fabric. Hem depth is another factor—both your height and the fashion fabric influence the choice of finished hem depth. Generally, a tall woman requires a slightly deeper hem, and a short woman a narrower hem.

A very full, sheer skirt with a hemline on the straight grain can have a hem up to 10" (25.5cm) deep if you want it to influence the drape of the fabric. A fabric like chiffon can have a narrow ⅛" (3mm) hem. A circular skirt usually calls for a hem no deeper than 1" (25mm). Jackets and pants may have a 1½" (3.8cm) hem; blouses may have from ⅜" to 1½" (10mm to 38mm), depending on style. In a very heavy fabric, avoid a deep hem no matter what the sweep of the skirt is. Such a hem may distort the drape and interfere with the silhouette.

Make sure your garment has time to hang before finalizing the hem—overnight is usually sufficient. Flared or circular skirts; garments made of crepe, chiffon, knits, and stretch fabrics; and garments cut on the bias need 24 hours to allow the fabric and any bias seams to relax. Otherwise you may have a sagging, uneven finished hem.

Before finalizing your hem, experiment with its length with everything in place. Insert pins at right angles to the raw hem edge and pin the hem at different lengths until you find the one that is right for you, the design, and your accessories. Check the length of a straight fitted skirt while sitting as well.

Use pins, chalk, or a combination of these; adjust the skirt marker to your needs. For accuracy, have someone else mark your hem, moving around you while you stand still. Place pins every 3" (7.5cm) for straight skirts and every 2" (5cm) for flared skirts.

After the hemline has been marked, thread-trace it and pin up the hem again; place pins at right angles to the raw hem edge, using pins as needed so the hem falls naturally. The hem should be parallel to the floor regardless of length.

The Final Touches

You have handled your garment with expert care throughout the fitting and construction process. Your garment should be close to perfection as you approach the final touches with the same zest and exuberance with which you began your project.

THE SHAPEKEEPERS

Snaps, hooks and eyes, lingerie strap guards, waistline stays, and weights are all examples of small details that can make a big difference in the final fit of your garment. They are details that make your garment truly special.

Snaps or hooks and eyes

The careful positioning of a snap or hook and eye at places such as the corner of a neckline, inside the underlap of a wrap dress, or at the end of a waistband extension can enhance the appearance and improve the fit by removing stress and maintaining the proper drape of the garment.

  With your garment in place on your body you can determine the correct position for any necessary snaps or hooks and eyes. Pin the garment in place and with another pin or marking pencil mark the corresponding fabric layer.

Weights

Weights are used to preserve the design lines of a garment and to prevent it from shifting during wear, thus preserving the perfected fit of your garment. They are most commonly used in the hemlines of coats and in the drape of a cowl.

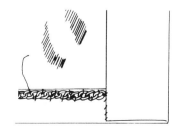

Waistline stays

This reinforcement is used at the waistline of garments with a waistline seam, those made of stretchy fabrics, fitted sheath or princess designs, or those where the skirt is heavier than the bodice. A stay will preserve the fit of the garment by preventing it from shifting during wear. Information on adding a waistline stay to your garment can be found on page 139.

Lingerie strap guards

These small guards are used to prevent the shoulder seams from shifting and keep lingerie straps from showing. They are extremely helpful with large open necklines or loose-fitting tops.

  Use about 1½" (3.8cm) of seam binding or a thread chain. Sew one end to the shoulder seam near the armhole. Sew a ball snap to the free end of the guard and a socket snap to the shoulder seam near the neck edge.

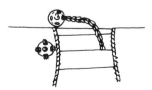

PRESSING

A careful touch-up press ensures a lasting perfect fit in your fashion garment. Any remaining small wrinkles and tiny puckers will disappear with a bit of attention at the ironing board.

If you have regularly pressed the garment throughout all phases of construction, any pressing at this point will be minimal, but may well be crucial for a precise fit. It cannot, however, be expected to resolve fitting problems that have been neglected.

Use all the pressing tools at your disposal to transform your flat ironing board into a three-dimensional platform on which you can apply this finishing touch. Improvise if you do not have a tool that would be helpful. If you have a dress form, use it now to spot-steam the roll of a collar and lapel, a patch pocket or sleeve caps as you refine your fashion just as you used it to help with alterations.

Pressing techniques depend on the particular fabric and garment construction, but there are some basic rules that should always be followed.

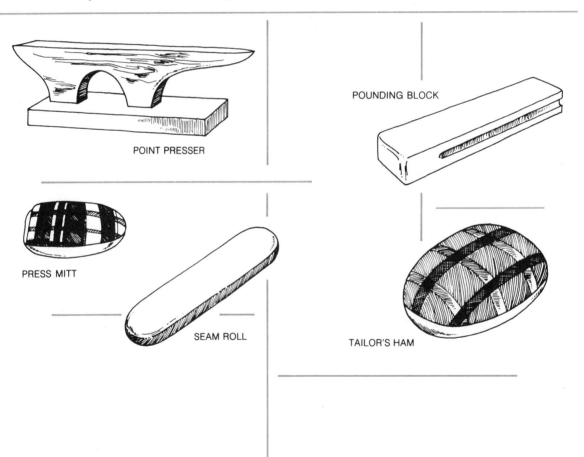

POINT PRESSER

POUNDING BLOCK

PRESS MITT

SEAM ROLL

TAILOR'S HAM

□ Have an assortment of equipment available so that you can place the fabric in the most practical position for the area being pressed.

□ Test a scrap of fabric to determine the proper heat setting for your iron.

□ Check your fabric's reaction to steam and moisture. Water marks, puckerings, or dulling may result if this is neglected.

□ Press with the grain of the fabric whenever possible; be careful not to stretch edges or curves by pulling the fabric.

□ Whenever possible, press on the wrong side of the fabric. If you must press on the right side, use a press cloth.

□ Never press any sharp creases until the fit of your garment has been completed.

□ To avoid marring the fabric, do not press over basting threads or pins.

□ Know your fabric—do not overpress.

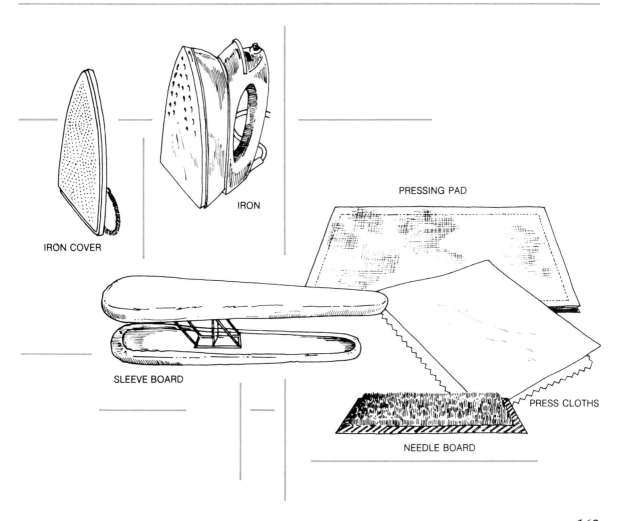

IRON

IRON COVER

PRESSING PAD

SLEEVE BOARD

PRESS CLOTHS

NEEDLE BOARD

6   *Fitting Pants*

Pants are a staple in almost every woman's wardrobe. They can be casual, tailored, or elegant and can be worn from morning through evening. There are pants designed for every occasion and created in a variety of fabrics, influenced by both fashion and function. As you gain knowledge about fit and your body, you will be able to choose with confidence the styles that will flatter your figure.

Your goal is to create pants that are comfortable, attractive, and beautifully constructed—the basic elements of good fit. Because of the nature of pants and the endless variations of body shapes, they demand precise attention to fitting details. A bit of time and effort invested in measuring and adjusting will result in a refined fit that will flatter your figure.

Your figure may require only minor adjustments to achieve a perfect fit, but if you find your body contours demand some special attention, you may want to make a pants fitting shell first. Whether you make a fitting shell or proceed directly to your fashion fabric, the information on the following pages will guide you through the steps for creating pants you will be proud to wear.

To make a fitting shell, use Vogue Pants Fitting Shell #1798. It includes a tissue pattern for the basic pants style plus instructions for adjusting and altering a fitting shell.

Creating Illusions

The shape of the pants you wear can have a tremendous effect on your overall silhouette. Select your patterns carefully, choosing designs that are best for your figure type. If you have prominent hips, a hip-hugging style with tapered legs would not only be difficult to fit, but would also be unflattering. A softly pleated loose-fitting pattern with a straight leg would be a much better choice. If you have a flat derriére, a design with a touch of fullness is a better choice than one that is closely tailored.

The illusions created by specific design features are crucial factors that can make or break the image you want to create.

SILHOUETTE

At all times you should strive for a balanced silhouette. A long jacket, tunic, or top can camouflage those few extra pounds or inches or give an illusion of height. If you are short, you may prefer a shorter top to preserve a pleasing proportion.

The amount of fullness designed into pants varies greatly with fashion trends and the function of the garment. Active sportswear, such as tennis shorts or jogging pants, would require more fullness than casual pants. Elegant evening pants are often designed with excess fullness for a special fashion effect.

A full silhouette will often add inches, so if your body is slim, a full-cut design will create a flattering illusion. But if you are already carrying some extra inches, fullness will only exaggerate the situation.

On the other hand, a close-fitting silhouette will expose figure characteristics that you may prefer to hide. If you are not one of the few with a "perfect figure," a good basic pants design with enough fullness to be comfortable for its purpose and to allow the fabric to fall smoothly over your body contours is the most flattering choice.

LINE

The position of the construction seams creates lines that can emphasize or camouflage unflattering figure characteristics. Vertical seams down the front and/or back of the pants leg (see seam fitting, page 185) create an illusion of height or slimness by cutting the width of the leg. A crisply pressed crease has the same effect.

Horizontal seams tend to broaden the body. A slim-hipped body can profit by an illusion of fullness with a yoke seam, whereas a yoke seam on a body with full hips will create an unflattering appearance.

LENGTH

The overall length of your pants is determined by the design, which varies from the shortest of shorts to a length barely touching the floor. The most important consideration is to make certain your pants do not end at an unflattering point on your leg. Sometimes even an adjustment of ½" (13mm) can make a world of difference in the overall impression.

Figures with heavy thighs should avoid shorts that end at the full thigh. A longer length will often camouflage and be more attractive.

Your height will also influence the choice of pants length. A longer pant leg will suggest greater height, thus often a more flattering image.

The best way to determine a flattering length is to experiment. When you cut your pants, allow enough additional length to raise and lower the hemline. Examine the results in a full-length mirror and choose a length that creates an appearance pleasing to your eye and to your figure.

Taking Measurements

As you prepare to measure your body for pants, it is important to choose proper undergarments. What you wear under your pants can make a big difference in their overall fit and appearance. Select undergarments that enhance your figure and avoid those that create lines or bulges.

Waist Tie a string around your body, letting it settle comfortably at the waistline. Measure your waist at the string (1).

High hip Measure across the top of the hip bones 2" to 4" (5cm to 10cm) below the waist (2).

Full hip Measure the fullest part of your hips, which should be 7" to 9" (18cm to 23cm) below the waist, depending on your figure type (3).

Leg circumference Measure the fullest part of the thigh, knee, calf, and instep (4, 5, 6, 7).

Pants length Measure at the side from the waist to floor or to the desired length. Pants length will vary with style and fashion; use your pattern and your good judgment as a guide when measuring finished length.

Crotch depth Sit on a hard chair and measure along your side from the string at your waist to the chair seat (9).

Crotch length Slide a large paper clip or safety pin onto a tape measure so that the clip moves freely. Place the tape measure between your legs and position the paper clip at the midpoint of your body (the lowest point). Determine the front and the back crotch length by measuring from the back waist to the clip and continuing to the front waist. This is not usually an even distribution and, therefore, becomes an important measurement for a perfect pants fit (10).

Torso length This measurement is necessary only for jumpsuits and requires two tape measures, or a long piece of seam tape or string which you can use and measure afterward. Measure from the string at your center front waistline over the fullness of your bust to the middle of your shoulder; continue down to your center back waistline under the crotch and back up to the center front waist (11).

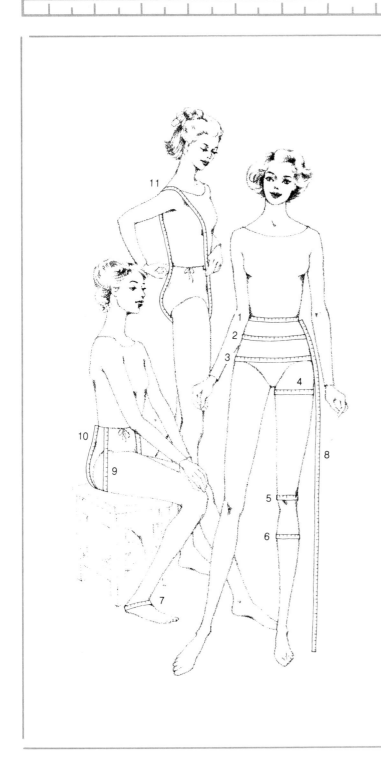

1 _____

2 _____

3 _____

4 _____

5 _____

6 _____

7 _____

8 _____

9 _____

10 _____

11 _____

Selecting a Pattern Size

After you have taken your measurements, compare them with the standard body measurements to find your best pattern size. Select a fitted pants pattern by your waist measurement; if your hip measurement is much larger or smaller in proportion to your waist, select the pattern closer to your hip measurement and adjust the waist. Pants with an elasticized waist finish should be purchased in the size closest to your hip measurement, since you may be able to avoid a waist adjustment entirely if the differences are minor. Jumpsuits should be purchased in the size you would normally use for a blouse or dress.

167

Pattern Tissue Adjustments

The next step toward a perfect pants fit is to compare your personal measurements to the pattern and determine the pattern tissue adjustments that are necessary. This must be done carefully, keeping wearing and design ease in mind (see pages 33–34), and using your own common sense.

LENGTH ADJUSTMENTS

Since your pants may reveal curves you would rather conceal, it is especially important to bring them vertically into proportion with you. This must be done before cutting out your fabric, as incorrect crotch and leg length are impossible to remedy. Refer back to pages 40–42 for general information regarding lengthening and shortening adjustments.

Pants length can be adjusted in three crucial areas: the crotch depth, the crotch length, and the overall length of the pants. One adjustment will definitely affect the others, so proceed with caution. Start with the crotch depth, then the crotch length, and finally the overall length.

The crotch depth is adjusted along the lengthening or shortening line below the waist. The crotch length is adjusted along the center front and/or center back of the pants at the crotch seam. The overall length is adjusted on the pants leg along a lengthening or shortening line or along the bottom edge, depending on the design of the pants.

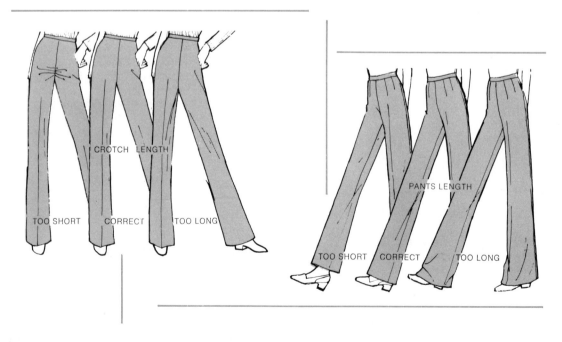

Crotch depth

Measure and adjust the crotch
depth before you measure the
crotch length or the overall
pants length. Establish a crotch
line if none is given on the
back pattern. Draw a line perpendicular to the grainline
across the width of the pattern
at the lowest point of the
crotch seamline. This will also
be the widest part of the pattern. Measure the back pattern
piece from the waistline to the
crotch line near the side seamline. Crotch depth should
exactly equal your established
crotch depth measurement plus
½" to ¾" (13mm to 20mm) for
wearing ease. Patterns with a
yoke or contour waistband
must be measured from the
waistline including the additional pattern piece. Match
notches and measure as usual,
excluding seam allowances.
Pants patterns that do not extend up to the natural waistline
must be compared with a regular pattern to determine
where the natural waistline is
located above the pattern.
  Make any necessary length
adjustments along the marked
adjustment line. To shorten,
fold out excess length; to
lengthen, slash and spread the
amount needed over tissue paper. Pin, check the adjustment,
and secure with tape. Redraw
the seamlines, making a
smooth crotch curve. Make an
equal adjustment on the front
pattern piece.

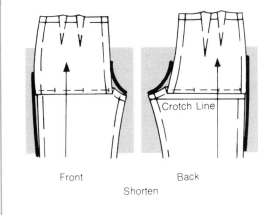

Front　　Back
Shorten

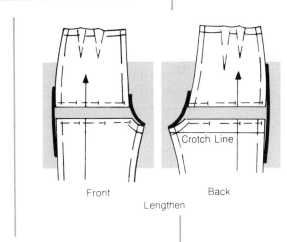

Front　　Back
Lengthen

169

Crotch length

With a tape measure on its side, follow the curve to measure from the waistline along the center front and center back seams, eliminating the seam allowances. Compare to your established measurement, allowing up to a total of 1½" (3.8cm) for wearing ease.

It is important to divide the total crotch length as needed at the front and the back. For example, a protruding derriere would require most or all of the adjustment length in the back. A protruding stomach would require most or all of the adjustment length on the pants front. Refer to your measurements for front crotch length and back crotch length to de-

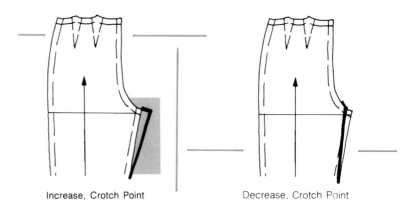

Increase, Crotch Point   Decrease, Crotch Point

termine where your adjustment(s) should be.

To add length, measure and mark the amount of the increase at the crotch seam. Redraw the inseam from the corrected point at the crotch, tapering to the original line at the knee.

To remove length, measure and mark the amount of the decrease from the crotch seam. Redraw the inseam from the corrected point at the crotch, tapering to the original line at the knee.

Torso length

Measure both front and back pattern pieces. Begin at the middle of the shoulder seam and measure to the waistline marking; exclude any blousing allowances, which should be marked on the pattern. Continue along the center front and center back seams to the crotch points. Add the front and back measurements and compare it to your torso measurement, allowing up to 2" (5cm) for wearing ease. Jumpsuit patterns with a waistline seam can be handled as two separate units, a bodice and pants.

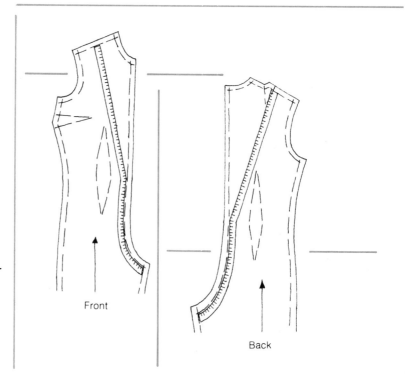

Front

Back

170

Pants length

Determine whether length adjustment should be made at the lower edge or above the knee to preserve style lines. Draw a line as you did to establish the position lines. Use your side length measurement from waist to hemline to determine the need for adjustment.

Shorten by folding out excess along the adjustment line. Lengthen by slashing and spreading the amount needed over tissue paper. Pin, check the adjustment, and secure with tape. Redraw the seamlines.

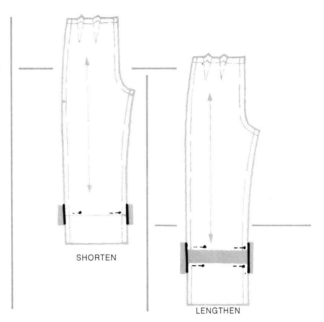

SHORTEN

LENGTHEN

Additional pattern markings

Mark any adjustment and fitting lines on your pattern tissue that aren't already there: Start with the front pattern piece and extend the grainline the full length of the pattern. Draw lines perpendicular to the grainline at the points where your high hip, full hip, and thigh fall. Measure down from the waist just as you did on your body. For slim pants it may be necessary to mark the knee and calf positions as well.

Extend the grainline on the back pattern piece. Lay the back pattern piece over the front, matching the sides at the notches. Indicate the position of each line and draw coordinating lines on the back pattern piece perpendicular to the grainline.

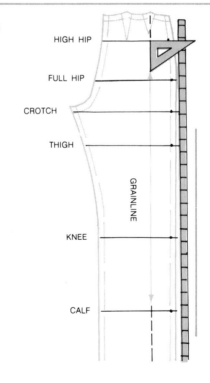

HIGH HIP

FULL HIP

CROTCH

THIGH

GRAINLINE

KNEE

CALF

CIRCUMFERENCE ADJUSTMENTS

Even though pants patterns are purchased by the waist measurement, some additional circumference adjustments may be necessary. Pants, which hide very little, must lie smoothly to fit well and comfortably. Your measurements, taken accurately and compared with the standard body measurements, will determine both the location and the extent of any adjustment needed.

Measure all the pattern pieces from seamline to seamline, excluding any darts or tucks. If the pants have a side front slanted pocket, be sure to include the side front pattern piece.

For the waist and hip, first compare your body measurements with the standard body measurements for your size listed on the pattern envelope. If these differ, you will have to make pattern adjustments. Next compare your high hip and full hip measurements with the pattern to see if additional hip alterations are necessary for your figure. Measure the pattern at the thigh position and compare it to your measurements. The pattern should equal your thigh measurement plus at least 1" (25mm) for wearing ease.

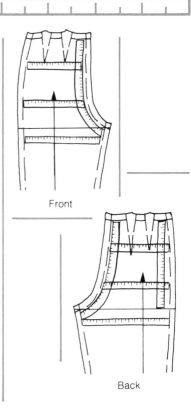

Front

Back

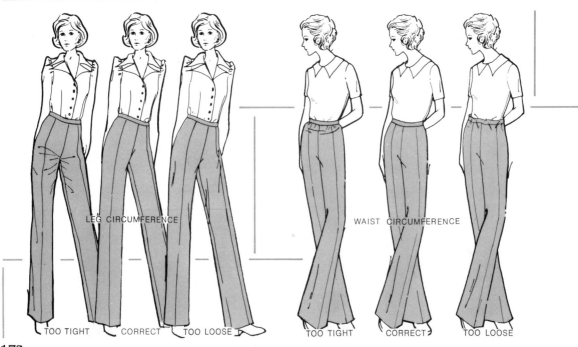

LEG CIRCUMFERENCE   WAIST CIRCUMFERENCE

TOO TIGHT   CORRECT   TOO LOOSE   TOO TIGHT   CORRECT   TOO LOOSE

Hip circumference

Basic circumference adjustments must be made before you cut your fabric. Then you can alter your pants for specific figure characteristics such as large or small buttocks or a protruding abdomen after your first fitting. These adjustments are described on pages 176–183. It is impossible to evaluate and perfect your pants fit without a properly fitted hip circumference, so measure and adjust carefully and precisely.

Compare your hip measurement to the standard hip measurement for your size given on the pattern envelope. Make the hip adjustment along the side seam on both front and back pattern pieces, making one-fourth of the total adjustment at each seam.

To increase, measure and mark the adjustment at the hipline. Redraw the cutting line, tapering to the original line at the waist and thigh.

To decrease, measure and mark the adjustment at the hipline. Redraw the cutting line, tapering to the original line at the waist and thigh.

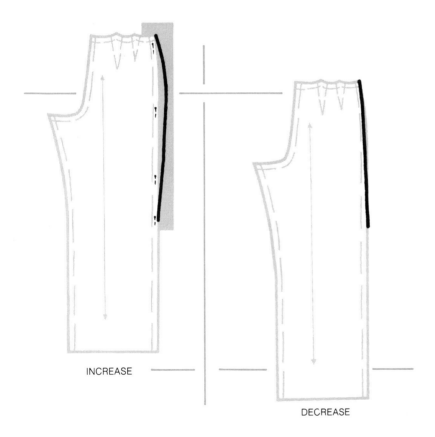

INCREASE

DECREASE

Leg circumference

Compare your thigh measurement plus 1″ (25mm) wearing ease to the measurement from seamline to seamline just below the crotch line on both the back and front pattern pieces. To reduce, mark one-half of the amount needed at the inner leg seam as shown. To enlarge, add tissue paper to the inner seam and crotch area and mark one-half of the amount needed. Draw new cutting lines, tapering to the original ones. Make certain that you maintain the crotch curve.

If you are making tapered, slim-fitted pants, check your knee, calf, and instep measurements, adding at least 1″ (25mm) wearing ease to each measurement. Measure from seamline to seamline along coordinating positions on both front and back pattern pieces. Reduce or enlarge circumferences as for the thigh.

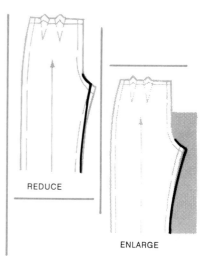

REDUCE

ENLARGE

Waist circumference

Small adjustments, up to 2″ (5cm), can be made at the side seams. Mark one-fourth of the adjustment needed at the side seams of both the front and back pattern pieces. Large adjustments, over 2″ (5cm), should be distributed evenly among center and side seams: mark one-eighth of the adjustment needed at each seam on both front and back pieces.

To decrease, measure and mark the adjustment. Redraw the cutting lines, tapering from the adjusted waist to the full hip.

To increase, measure and mark the adjustment, adding tissue paper if necessary. Redraw the cutting lines, tapering from the adjusted waist to the full hip.

Make corresponding adjustments on all facings, waistbands, or other waistline finishes. Pants with an elasticized waist should not need a waist adjustment.

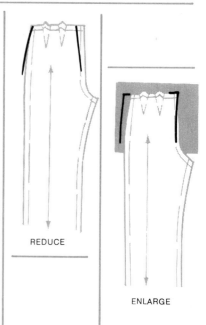

REDUCE

ENLARGE

The Pants Fitting Shell

You now have all the facts necessary for basic length and circumference adjustments— the first step toward a perfect pants fit. But if you have a figure that requires a bit of extra attention, you may want to make some of the additional adjustments described in the following pages. If you have a fair understanding of your body and have had experience with other pants patterns, you may want to proceed with the necessary adjustments directly on your fashion fabric. On the other hand, if you are experimenting with pants fitting, or if you want to create a permanent pants pattern, you may want to make a pants fitting shell.

A fitting shell is sewed in muslin or gingham from Vogue's Pants Fitting Shell #1798 for the sole purpose of solving fitting problems. After the shell has been altered to fit you perfectly, the adjustments you have made are transferred to your Vogue pattern tissue. The adjusted tissue then becomes your permanent pattern.

The development of a permanent pants pattern will provide you with a perfect sewing tool, saving you time and trouble whenever you sew. You will use it with each new style you make to adjust the pattern before cutting the fabric, thus avoiding costly mistakes.

Once you have a pants pattern that has been fitted perfectly to your body proportions refer to page 104 for information on making your pattern permanent.

MAKING THE PANTS FITTING SHELL

The classic pants fitting shell is a closely fitted pants pattern with darts, a waistband, back zipper, and straight-cut legs. Vogue's Pants Fitting Shell #1798 is specifically designed for this purpose, with all the features and special instructions necessary to help you achieve a personalized fit and a perfect permanent pattern. Refer to page 62 for information on selecting and preparing the fabric for your fitting shell.

Adjust the Vogue Pants Fitting Shell #1798 to your measurements, and arrange the fabric as indicated on the cutting layout. Pin the selvages together, matching your crosswise grain markings. The fabric must be perfectly on grain before you pin the pattern pieces to it. Cut out your muslin shell carefully; even the addition of ⅛" (3mm) can distort the fit.

As you begin your pants fitting it can be helpful to cut the seam allowances a bit wider, to allow you to make changes and still have adequate fabric for the seam allowance. Just make certain that you mark and stitch the seamlines accurately.

Using a tracing wheel and dressmaker's tracing paper, transfer all construction and position lines from the fitting pattern to your muslin. Mark seamlines, darts, hipline, and crotch line. Seamlines and darts should be marked on the wrong side of the fabric; mark the hipline and crotch line on the right side. It is also helpful to mark the grainline on the right side if you are using muslin rather than gingham fabric.

Follow the pattern sewing instructions when making your fitting shell. Stitch the garment sections together with machine basting or a chainstitch so changes can be made easily. Stitch seam tape to the waistline to prevent stretching, and machine baste the zipper in place.

Any adjustments you need to make must be done with care and forethought. Begin with changes in the crotch depth and crotch length; proceed with any additional adjustments in the circumference, beginning with the waist and working down. Be aware of the chain reaction these changes can cause. Proceed cautiously when making any permanent changes. Refer to pages 114–115 for specific information on the technique of altering a garment on your body and transferring those changes to your tissue pattern.

175

SHAPING THE PANTS FITTING SHELL

By making the pattern tissue adjustments, you have brought the fitting shell into proportion with your figure. Because they are based on measurements alone, these adjustments cannot be expected to accommodate the body curves that are unique to you. If your adjusted fitting shell has not passed the visual and physical tests of fit under careful scru-

tiny, you will want to continue the fitting process to resolve those problems that are related to your individual contours. Through these further alterations you can achieve a basic fitting shell in which perfect fit is a reality and which will be your fundamental sewing tool.

The most important aspect of altering your pants shell is to understand your individual

body contours. The following pages provide information on the cause, effect, and solution of a range of problems flowing from specific figure charac-teristics. It may be helpful to analyze the fit of other pants you have made or purchased as you attempt to determine which alterations will help you toward your goal of a perfect fit.

Large abdomen

A large abdomen distorts the whole front of your pants from the crotch to the waist because not enough fabric has been al-lowed to accommodate your contour. Strain at the crotch and inseam as well as crosswise wrinkles appearing below the waist can be elimi-nated by extending the length of the front crotch seam. Re-lease the waist, inseam, and darts, and drop the top of the pants until the side seams fall into position. Add a strip of fabric to the top of the pants and to the front inner leg seam of your fitting shell if neces-sary. Pin the darts to fit the contour of your body. Transfer the alteration to your front pat-tern piece.

For styles with front pleats or pants with an elasticized waist, alter in the same manner. Jumpsuits with a one-piece bodice and pants will require slashing across the waist to the middle of each front section, and then diagonally to the knee to get the extra length needed.

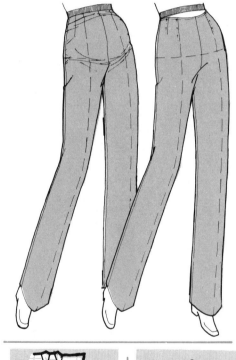

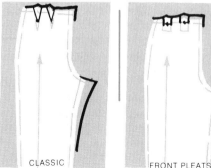

CLASSIC

FRONT PLEATS

JUMPSUIT

176

Protruding hip bones

This figure characteristic, caused by bone structure, creates pulling and wrinkling over the high hip area. To correct, release the darts and repin to fit your contour. Depending on your bone structure, shorten or widen the darts as necessary. If this makes the waistline smaller, add the necessary amount to the side seams. Transfer the alteration to the front pattern piece.

For pants with a pleated front, alter in the same manner. This alteration is not usually necessary for pants with elasticized waists. To alter jumpsuits with a one-piece bodice and pants, slash to the center of the pattern and then diagonally to the knee to give you extra width to fit darts.

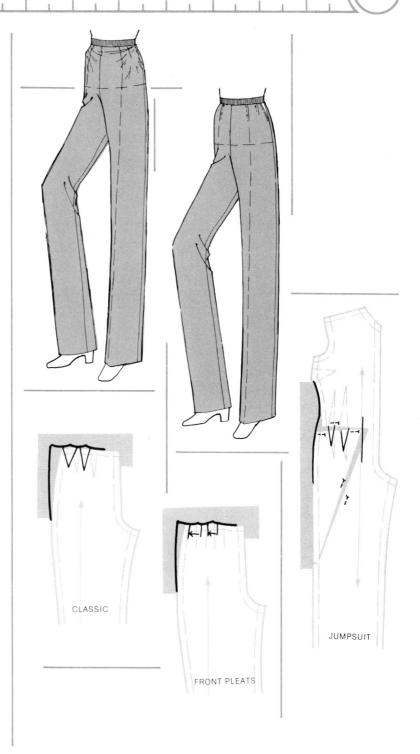

CLASSIC

FRONT PLEATS

JUMPSUIT

177

Swayback

As a result of posture, bone structure, or excess weight, many women have a swayback. It is as apparent in pants as in a skirt: the same wrinkling occurs below the waistline at the back. To correct, pin out the excess fabric, tapering the fold to the side seams. Release and repin the darts, reducing their length. Transfer the alteration to the pattern tissue at the center back.

Make the same alterations on pants with an elasticized waist and redraw the casing foldline. For pants with a back yoke, reduce the yoke pattern piece at the center back. To alter a jumpsuit with a one-piece bodice and pants, slash at the waist and lap the amount needed to shorten the center back length. Redraw the leg and grainline as illustrated.

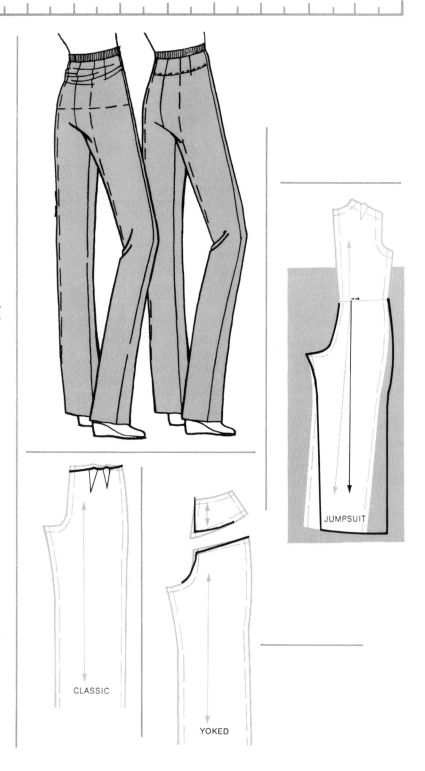

CLASSIC

YOKED

JUMPSUIT

High hip

Many women develop one high hip as a result of carrying books, groceries, or babies on one side. This figure characteristic causes the pants to hang off grain and creates diagonal pulls from the crotch to the hip. You cannot proceed with the pants fitting until this condition is corrected. Pull the pants down on the high side until the grain falls evenly and the pulls disappear. The alteration will require additional length on the high side of your body. Remark the new waist seamline, adding fabric to your fitting shell if necessary. Transfer the alteration to the front and back pattern pieces. When cutting a double thickness of fabric, it will be easier to cut the fabric for the high side and trim the excess from the low side before applying the waistband.

Pants with pleats and elasticized waists are adjusted in the same manner. Jumpsuits with a one-piece bodice and pants need a separate pattern for the left and right side. Trace a new pattern piece and adjust for the high side by slashing at the waist and spreading the amount needed. Redraw the leg and grainline as illustrated.

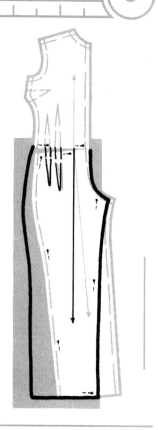

Low buttocks

Pants that tend to pull down in the back when sitting are often a result of low buttocks. To alter, you will need to lower the back crotch curve. Lower the seam by tapering from nothing at the back notches to the adjusted amount to nothing again at the inseam. You will need to clip in order to determine the correct amount, so lower the curve only a small amount at a time until you determine the amount of adjustment you need for a smooth-fitting back. Transfer the total alteration to the back pattern piece.

Pants with an elasticized waist and jumpsuits are altered in the same manner.

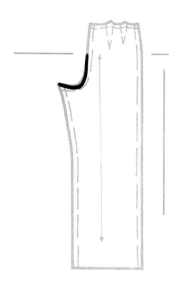

179

Flat buttocks

Wrinkles form at the buttocks area, and the pants sag because the body lacks the contour to support the fullness. To alter, pin out the excess along the high hipline and down each leg. Taper folds to nothing at the side seams, waist, and knee. Release the waist darts and repin them to fit the body curves; work out the extra waist circumference at the side seams. Transfer the alteration to the back pattern piece.

 Pants that feature an elasticized waist and pants with a back yoke are altered in the same manner. For jumpsuits with one-piece bodice and pants, slash at the waist and lap the amount needed to reduce the back length. Starting at the slash, fold out excess girth, and taper to the knees. Redraw the leg and grainline as illustrated.

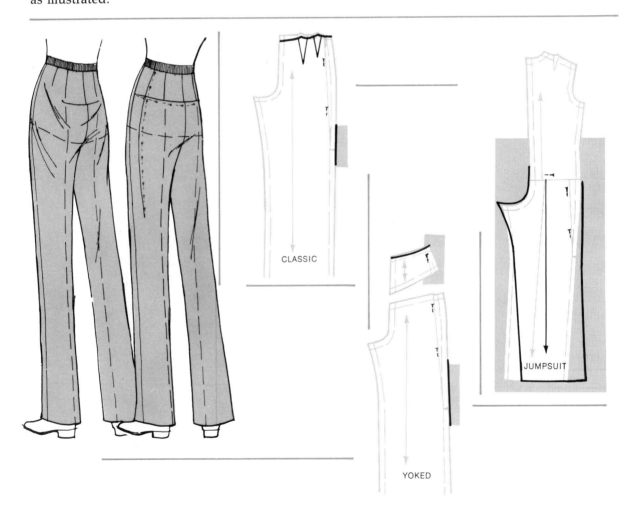

CLASSIC

YOKED

JUMPSUIT

Large buttocks

While the hip circumference of your pants will have been accommodated by your flat pattern adjustments, large buttocks may require more fabric for the pants to fit properly and comfortably. Also, the contours of the front of your body may take away needed girth. The pants will pull down across the back, and the side seams and inseams will wrinkle and strain through the hip area. To correct, remove the stitching from the darts and release the inseams to the knee. Lower the top of the pants into position, and, if necessary, add strips of fabric to the top of the fitting shell so the pants reach the waist. Also add to the back inseams until the pants drape smoothly. Pin darts to fit the shape of the body, and increase the waist at the side seams if needed. Transfer the alteration to the pattern tissue as shown.

   Make the same alteration on pants with an elasticized waist and redraw the casing foldline. Alter pants with a back yoke as shown. For jumpsuits with a one-piece bodice and pants, slash at the waist and then diagonally to the knee to get the extra length that is needed. Redraw the leg and grainline as illustrated.

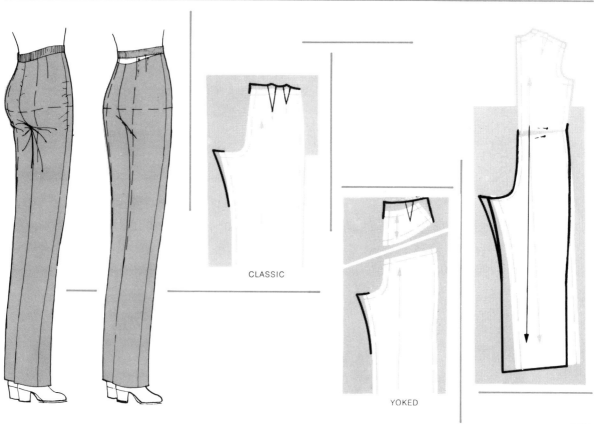

CLASSIC

YOKED

Thigh bulge

Many women have this figure characteristic regardless of their weight or posture. It appears below the full hipline and seems to be the widest point of the body even though circumference measurements of the hip might not agree. Crosswise wrinkles occur across the front and back of the pants from strain at the side seams and inseams. Release the stitching at the side seams and spread the amount needed until the wrinkles disappear and the pants legs hang smoothly. Insert strips of fabric under the edges of the fitting shell if needed.

When transferring the alteration to the pattern pieces, divide the amount equally between the front and back pattern pieces. At the widest point of the thigh bulge, slash the pattern from the side seam approximately 3" (7.5cm) into the garment. Slash from the innermost point to the knee. Any style of pants, as well as jumpsuits with one-piece bodice and pants, can be altered in this way.

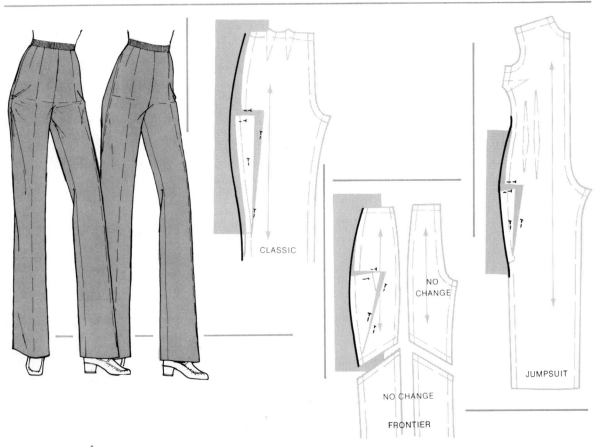

CLASSIC

NO CHANGE

NO CHANGE

FRONTIER

JUMPSUIT

Thin thighs

On a figure with thin thighs, pants have excess vertical full-ness in the back between the legs. To correct, pin out the ex-cess along the back inseam until the pants fall smoothly. If the pants are full in the front, you may have to remove some fabric from the front inseam as well. Transfer the alteration to the pattern pieces along the in-seam, tapering to nothing at the knee area.

Pants with an elasticized waist and jumpsuits are altered in the same manner.

Puckered darts

Darts are formed to shape fabric around body fullness; those that are not positioned properly will not lie smoothly over the body contours. Sometimes the problem can be corrected by merely shortening or lengthening the dart. Alter the length on the pants and correct the tissue pattern accordingly. A dart can also be moved to the right or left to accommodate the body contours and correct the fit. If protruding hip bones are the cause, refer to page 177 for the proper adjustment.

Many times an alternative solution for front darts is to form small tucks or pleats in place of the darts.

Smile lines

Pants with a crotch seam that is too short for the body will have wrinkles pointing upward from the crotch seam. If the problem is minor, an adjustment can be made in the crotch seam. Lengthen the crotch by lowering the curve gradually in the area between the front and back notches up to ⅜" (10mm) at the inseam. Adjust the tissue pattern accordingly. If the problem is major, refer to the adjustments for crotch length and crotch depth on pages 169–170.

Smile lines can also be caused by other fitting problems such as heavy thighs. If the strain appears to be coming from the thigh rather than the crotch seam, refer to page 182 for information on the adjustment for heavy thighs.

Frown lines

Pants with a crotch seam that is too long for the body will have wrinkles pointing downward from the crotch seam. An adjustment can be made along the crotch seam if the problem is minor. Shorten the crotch by raising the curve gradually in the area between the front and back notches an amount up to ⅜" (10mm) at the inseam. Adjust the tissue pattern accordingly. If the problem is major, refer to the adjustments for crotch length and crotch depth on pages 169–170.

Frown lines can also be caused by other fitting problems such as thin thighs. If this appears to be the cause, refer to page 183 for information on the adjustment for thin thighs.

Seam fitting

A more stylized way to alter pants is to contour the backs of the legs with seam fitting, or to taper the legs at each side seam and inseam.

Contouring the backs of the legs is a combined fitting technique and styling feature. You can use it to create closely fitted pants. On each leg of your muslin, pin out the excess fabric from the back dart closest to the center down to the hem; try to keep the seam parallel to the grainline and in a straight line down the center back of each leg. Reshape the darts to your particular needs. Make an effort to preserve the style lines of your pants, even though the seam will vary in depth as it follows the shape of your body.

Transfer the new seamlines to your pattern. Remember that pants with flaring legs are not always on the straight grain below the knee; for these, keep the lower part of the new seam at the center of the leg.

Tapering is another technique for customizing pants. First, note the knee marking on your muslin. For snugly fitted pants legs, take in the side and inseams. Do not fit the knee area too tightly, as the pants would wear out more quickly. Divide the amount to be reduced between the two seams, tapering to the crotch and hip. Make sure to leave ample circumference at knee and instep.

To alter the pattern, mark one-fourth of the amount to be taken in at the hemline of each seam. Evenly draw new cutting lines from the hem up to the knee and then taper to the crotch and along the side seam. Taper pants with flaring legs gradually from the hemline to the knee; then taper both seams as above.

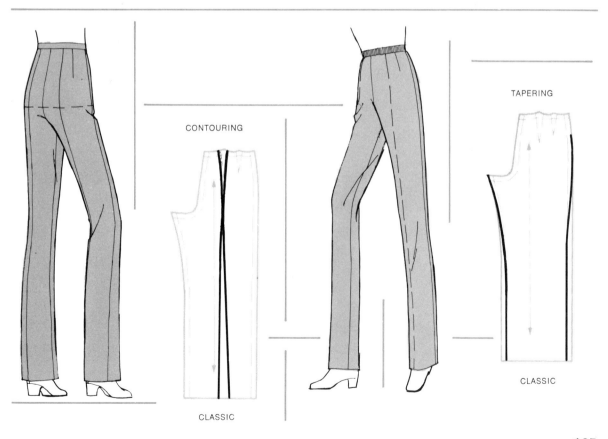

CONTOURING

CLASSIC

TAPERING

CLASSIC

Refining the Fit

By this point in the fitting process you should have pants that are well proportioned to your body contours. As you evaluate the fit of your pants, review the guidelines on page 187. Certain other factors, such as the fabric, the design, and your personal preferences, will determine whether any final minor refinements are necessary.

Fabric can alter the fit of your pants. Understanding the characteristics of special fabrics can help you make the minor adjustments that might be needed. Many fabrics are not suitable for pants, and many designs require special fabric types to achieve the intended look. The pattern envelope will include information on fabrics suitable for the specific design. For information on fitting techniques useful for different types of fabric, refer to pages 24–25.

Design variations will require different criteria for the final fit. Obviously harem pants should not fit like jeans, and tailored suit pants should not fit like jogging pants. The pattern envelope will describe the intended fit. It is essential that you have a complete understanding of wearing and design ease as you proceed to refine your fit. Regardless of the design, you would still make all necessary personal adjustments. You may find the harem pants a bit more flattering with less fullness, or the jogging pants a little more comfortable with a longer crotch length. Limited refinements are still possible after your garment is cut and stitched; these alterations are determined after the major seams are stitched but before the final details are completed.

The length of the pants is often a major determinant of the style. A basic pants pattern can be cut in a variety of lengths and result in as many different pant styles. Short shorts and tailored suit pants could be cut from an identical pattern with the length being the determining style factor. Here you also have an opportunity to refine the fit. Adding a touch to the length of the shorts could result in a more flattering fit; adding a touch to the length of your tailored pants could refine the fit to perfection.

Evaluating the Fit

You must understand the elements of a good fit in order to achieve the results for which you are striving. Your pants should be comfortable, flattering, and beautifully constructed. These guidelines will help you evaluate your pants fit with an eye to perfection.

Always wear proper undergarments and shoes while fitting your pants; they will make a big difference. Stand, sit, and move while you are evaluating the fit: the pants must work with you and should always maintain the elements of a quality fit.

☐ Side seams and inseams should hang straight, perpendicular to the floor. From a side view, they should be centered on your leg.

☐ Horizontal position markings should be parallel to the floor.

☐ The lengthwise grainline should be straight and perpendicular to the floor.

☐ The waistband should fit comfortably around the natural waistline with enough wearing ease to be comfortable in all positions.

☐ Darts should fall smoothly over your figure, shaping the fabric to your body contours. A dart that is too short or too long will pucker—a minor adjustment is in order.

☐ The seat should fall smoothly around your hipline with enough wearing ease to move comfortably. A simple test is to be able to "pinch an inch" of fabric around the hip, allowing you 2" (5cm) of wearing ease.

☐ On the other hand, the seat should not be baggy, unless the specific pattern is designed in this manner. An unintended baggy seat needs some minor refinements in the fit.

☐ The crotch seam should follow the contour of your body and be smooth over its entire length. It should be the correct depth—neither high and binding, causing "smile" lines, nor low and baggy, causing "frown" lines.

☐ Each pants leg should hang smoothly and free from restrictions. There should be no strained areas. The "pinch an inch" test works well on the thigh area, too.

☐ The proposed hem length should be evaluated after the rest of your fitting is completed, and with shoes similar to those you intend to wear with the pants. The heel you wear makes a big difference in the finished length of your pants. Refer to Making a Permanent Pattern, page 104.

A Final Word

Congratulations once again! You have attained your goal of mastering the art of pattern fitting—an investment of time and energy that will continue to pay off with each new garment you sew.

You have made a complete analysis of your body, and have learned the intricacies of molding fashions to fit your figure and the pleasures of refining that fit to perfection. You have gained the knowledge and experience necessary to fit your patterns with ease and professionalism. Your creative role in fitting ends here. The time has come to wear your garment with the pride of knowing that you have given it all the attention necessary for a flawless fit.

Through all the ups and downs, the challenges and pitfalls, you have emerged victorious . . . the proud creator of a fashion garment that conforms beautifully to your figure, and that harmonizes all the elements of fabric, design, and fit. Now you can rest assured that the fitting techniques you have learned will never fail you, and your skill will improve with use.

Index

189

Dress pattern, 33
  enlargement at hips, 57–58
  enlargement at waist, 53–54
  lengthening of, 45
  reduction at hips, 55–56
  reduction at waist, 51–52
  shortening of, 43

Ease, 33–35
  distribution in sleeves, 73–74
Edges that meet, 113, 150
Elasticized sleeve finishes, 155
Elasticized waist finishes, 153
  of pants, 174
    and hip alterations, 179, 180, 181
    sway back alterations, 178
Elbows, thick, alteration of sleeve for, 78
Empire silhouette, 16
Enlargement of pattern:
  at hips, 57–58
  at waist, 53–54
Equipment for fitting, 28–29
Evaluation of fit, 116–121
  of pants, 187
Excess fabric, to remove, 115

Fabric amounts, 39
Fabric design, illusions created by, 17
Fabrics, 20–25
  for basic fitting shell, 62
  and gathers, 143
  and hem depth, 160
  and pants fit, 186
  and pattern size, 33
  seam allowances, 114
  special requirements of, 122–124
Facings, 158
  neckline, 127
  waistline, 153
Fibers, 20–21, 23
Figure problems, styles for, 19
Figure types, 31–32
Finishes of fabrics, 22
Fit:
  elements of, 11–17
  methods of, 26–28
  refinement of, 109–163
    for pants, 186
Fitted garments:
  bust adjustments, 82–88
  ease allowance, 34, 35
  lengthening of pattern, 45–46
  hip adjustments, 56
  pants, 175–185
  shortening of pattern, 43
  waist adjustments, 52, 54, 58
Fitting shell, 27, 61–108
  for pants, 164, 175–185
Flared leg pants, 185
Flax fibers, 20, 21

Forearms, alteration of sleeves for, 79, 80
French curve, 29
French darts, adjustments of, 47, 88
  for bust cup size, 82–87
  lengthening of pattern, 47
Frown lines of pants, 184
Full hip measurement, 30–31
  for pants, 166, 167
Fur-like fabrics, 24
Fusing of pattern to backing, 106

Gaping armholes, 72
Gaping neckline, alterations for, 69
Gathers, 142, 143
Geometric seaming, 131
Gored skirt, alterations to pattern, 52, 54, 56, 58
Grain of fabric, 21, 62
  distortion of, 120
  for pants, 187
  and pleats, 145
  of pocket, 152
  at shoulders, 63
  and underlining, 157
Grainlines, and adjustments to pattern, 39, 44
  to pants pattern, 171
Gusset, in kimono sleeve, 133

Halter neckline, 34, 70
  armhole area of, 71, 72
Hand basting, 111
Hand of fabric, 23
Harem pants, 186
Hem length, 18
Hemline:
  and abdominal alterations, 162, 163
  lengthening of pattern at, 45
  shortening of pattern at, 41
Hems, 121, 160
High bust measurement, 30–31
  and pattern size, 33
High hip measurement, 30–31
  for pants, 166, 167
High-waisted silhouettes, 16
Hip bones, protruding, 97, 140
  pants alterations for, 177
Hips:
  adjustments for, 97–101, 140–141
    enlargement of pattern, 57–58
    to lower, 45, 46
    for pants, 173, 177, 179
    to raise, 43
    reduction of pattern, 55–56
  measurement of, 30–31
  narrow, styles for, 14
Hooks and eyes, 161
Horizontal lines, 17
Horizontal seams, 120, 121
  of pants, 165
Horizontal wrinkles, 119

Illusions, flattering, 15, 17
In-seam closures, fitting of, 112
Inseams of pants, 187
Inset bands, 149
Interfacing, non-woven, pattern fused to, 106
Interrupted lines, redrawing of, 39, 40, 50
Ironing of garment, 162–163

Jacket:
  hem depth, 160
  length measurement, 31
  linings, 156
  patterns, 33, 35
    lengthening of, 45
    shortening of, 41, 43
Jewel neckline, 126
Jogging pants, 186
Jumpsuit:
  alterations to, 170
    for abdomen, 176
    for hips, 177, 179–181
    for sway back, 178
    for thighs, 182, 183
  measurements for, 166, 167
  pattern size for, 167

Kimono sleeves, 73
  adjustments to, 34, 133
    for arm shapes, 75, 77–80
    for back, 91–93, 95
    for bust cup size, 82, 84, 85
    for chest, 89–90
    at neckline, 68
    for shoulders, 64–67
Knit fabrics, 22, 24, 122
  darts in, 130
  facings, 158
  hems, 160
  neckline fitting, 127
  pocket placement, 152
  waist seam, 138
  zippers in, 150

Lace fabrics, 124
Lapped edges, 112
Layered fitting, 159
Leather-like fabrics, 25, 123
Leg circumference, 166, 167
  and alterations to pants, 174
Length, 13
  adjustments to pattern, 40–48
  of pants, 165, 186, 187
    adjustments to, 168–171
    measurements for, 166, 167
Lines:
  illusions created by, 17–18
  interrupted, redrawing of, 39, 40, 50
Lingerie strap guards, 161

190